MR THRIFTY'S

HOW TO SAVE MONEY ON ABSOLUTELY EVERYTHING

Updated edition of the cult guide
to smart living on less

JANE FURNIVAL

To the people of Scotland, with respect and admiration for teaching me a thing or two.

Jane Furnival lives with her family in a Gothic chapel needing considerable attention, in the cheapest part of South London. Here, she writes books and newspaper articles, on a diet of broken biscuits from the cheap shop across the road. Her hobby is eating chocolate.

First published in Great Britain in 2000 by
Mary Ford Books a division of Michael O'Mara Holdings
9 Lion Yard
Tremadoc Road
London SW4 7NQ

ISBN 1-85479-425-6

A CIP catalogue record for this book is available from the British Library.

3 5 7 9 10 8 6 4 2

Designed and typeset by Design 23

Printed and bound by Cox & Wyman Ltd, Reading, Berkshire

CONTENTS

Acknowledgements

Lesley O'Mara has all my gratitude for deciding that Mr Thrifty should re-open and ransack, once more, the treasury of his knowledge on the art of saving money.

Thanks also to Gabrielle Mander for shepherding the book to the press with much care, and to Nicola Paterson for her dogged research and Simon Tuite and Bryony Evens for picking up my mistakes..

Emma Soames and Richard Ingrams kindly asked me to write a magazine column under the name 'Mr Thrifty' in 1992. Then Susan Hill asked me to write the first Mr Thrifty book. I doff my hat deeply to her for suggesting the 'How to save money on absolutely everything' bit of the title.

I am indebted to everyone who has offered ideas. I have tried to name suggesters beside their suggestions, but apologise if I have left anyone out. On the home front, thanks as ever to Andy Tribble for fiddling with computers and Primrose Evans for all her help.

INTRODUCTION:
SAVE THE PRICE OF THIS BOOK

This book's aim is simple: to save you more than the money you paid for it.

Here you will find ideas, secrets and tricks of the trade to give you the best value on everything from boots to boilers, from flowers to funerals. In this revised and updated edition, I have also included high-price buys like houses and cars, hoping to save you thousands.

Since the first Mr Thrifty book appeared in 1994, I am delighted to say that thrift is no longer a word restricted to upper-class circles, where the Queen uses up her guests' soap-ends without, presumably, feeling it's a social comedown to economise. To keep the family seat going, the upper class has for years worn patched tweeds and lived in freezing rooms, while their dogs sat in privileged positions near the Aga.

We are now all in the same boat. Bargain-hunting has become a national sport, discussed openly. Who isn't affected by rising prices, especially after the privatisation of necessities like trains and water; by stealth taxes; and by the growing need to educate our children, then pay for our operations and provide for our old age, from our own pockets?

Mr Thrifty aims to save you money on life's boring bits, and get you things free if possible. I'm all in favour of treats, but this is not a book for hobbyist shoppers who automatically go shopping at weekends, and require an exhausting guide to every discount shop in Britain. I recommend many shops, but I don't equate value with cheapness. I would rather buy an expensive coat or pair of shoes which will last 20 years and still look good, like a Burberry which you can get retextured. Nor should you buy this book if you really want *What Vegetable Rack?* or similar nitpicking consumer publications, though I can tell you where to buy the best of these.

Thrift is a personal triumph. It is not the same as meanness at others' expense, like the man who saved money on two Christmas presents by buying a pair of slippers. He sent his two aunties one slipper each in torn paper, then told both that their other slipper was lost in the post.

Research is the key to thrift. I have saved you time by doing it for you. Before embarking on any long-winded money-saving scheme, like driving 200 miles to visit a particular shop, think: How much do I value my time per hour, and am I going to save more than this time's value, not to mention the cost of petrol? Otherwise, plump for purchasing something at a shop like John Lewis, with its famous promise: 'Never knowingly undersold'. For the best buys of the week, you can't do better than consult the excellent shopping and money sections of newspapers and magazines.

I have included some worldwide web addresses where they occurred naturally or offered a service worth having. But it's in the spirit of the first explorers of the New World. Computer shopping is not speedy. My first try at Internet shopping left me stuck for some hours in a Californian garage sale, where my computer had crashed. I felt like some science fiction character, alone and wandering a strange planet with a broken spaceship.

I don't believe that Internet shopping is the be-all and end-all of saving money. We hear of fabulous, distant bargains on the worldwide web, much as medieval people talked of huge sea-monsters. Braggarts who say they have bagged big bargains often ignore the cost of postage from abroad, and the time spent watching slowly-forming screens.

If you are short of time or not technically-minded, if you like talking to people, touching real things or enjoy the crackle of a mail-order catalogue between your fingers, you're not losing out by not surfing the net. If you're cyber-curious, try it out using a cyber-cafe, where you rent a machine by the hour and there are experts around to help, or the local library. Or even ask at a local school, rather than buy expensive equipment which crashes frequently, with inadequate support from a maker's helpline – candidates for a government regulator if ever there were (called OFFLINE, perhaps).

Thrift comes from simplicity. Don't buy more than you need. Don't be pushed into replacing old things with new, just because they're there. Fix it first. A bargain is only a bargain if you needed it when you left home for the shop. Don't waste shoe leather wandering idly around at 'discount outlet villages' which ruin our countryside, at the expense of high streets on your doorstep. A village should contain houses, a church, a shop-cum-post office and a pub, not a discount outlet; at these outlets you pay for petrol to get there, pay for parking, pay to eat... pay to pay.

You can curb an out-of-control shopping habit by getting things delivered. Somehow, brown paper parcels handed over by a gruff postman don't have the allure of shop assistants, tissue paper and crisp, glossy shop bags. After a few parcels, you won't feel so keen to buy things. Then you can go swimming, talk to a friend, or see a free museum exhibition instead.

It pays to complain of the shortcomings of companies. By fervent complaining, just over the last couple of years I have received a free luncheon for two from Liberty, a small Harrods hamper, bouquets from Barclays and American Express not to mention the odd £20 refund from Sky TV. Don't be intimidated. After sending repeated and insensitive bills to my late mother, the Television Licensing Authority received a letter from me suggesting that if they thought she was watching TV without a licence, they must dig her ashes up from the garden and ask her favourite programme. That elicited the very belated admission, from them, that her estate was due a refund.

Finally, extract entertainment value from thrift. There was a mass-murderess who was only caught because she couldn't resist making a patchwork quilt from her victim's trousers. Or take the case of the feisty Lady Amelia Noble-Johnson. To cater for a dinner party, she cannily purchased a pack of six pies at under £2 because it claimed '30 per cent more chicken pieces'. Judging them 'not as expected in terms of filling', she sued makers Freshbake Foods in Ipswich Magistrates Court. Freshbake explained that they did not mean there was more filling in their pies, merely that the chicken had been cut into 30 per cent more pieces. They received a £3500 fine.

I hope that you can use my suggestions to make ends meet – and meet so well that you will have enough left over to tie a huge curly-ended bow.

MR THRIFTY'S GUIDE TO SAVING MONEY EVERY TIME YOU STEP OUTSIDE YOUR FRONT DOOR

Ask: 'How much for cash?'

A magic formula. It works best if you first find the shop manager, or someone in authority. Junior staff are often too scared to lop money off, especially if there is a printed price tag.

Shawna Moss, a personal shopper who takes people on individual shopping trips, told me how her richest customer embarrasses her by asking for a reduction in the smartest shops if she pays cash. 'I hide behind the rails of coats!' she says. However this customer often gets considerable discounts. The shop is delighted with cash: it is spared the 3% cost of processing cheques or credit cards and waiting for the actual payment from the bank or card company.

Ask for a discount

You get over any embarrassment by giving them a reason why. Could you take it away then and there, or collect the thing yourself, saving them money on delivery? Is it slightly bashed? If, say, you are having curtains made, have you bought the fabric at the same shop? Are you a regular customer?

Ask: 'What's your best price?'
Smile as you say it. This phrase is worth its weight in gold.

Go back several times
You can wear down the dealer by returning a few times, then going away with furrowed brow but without the item. Never be haughty. Endear yourself. Say something like: 'It's wonderful, but not £100 wonderful' (or whatever the given price is). This strategy works best at unpretentious locations like car boot sales, worst in posh antique shops.

There is one breed of antique shop owner who hates parting with their stock at any price. Give up. Leave your phone number. I have occasionally received a call, several weeks after being told that whatever I wanted wasn't for sale, saying they made a mistake and it was for sale.

Go back just before closing time
This is the best way of getting bargains at car boot sales, supermarkets and other places where they want their stock off their hands as soon as possible.

Shop in high streets and markets, not malls

You save by shopping in less expensive areas of the country and especially our much-beleaguered high streets, rather than in shopping malls, which have huge overheads.

The shops aren't glamorous, but even supermarket chains lower their prices where people can't afford so much. Shop in Mayfair and you're hypnotised by wealth. After a while, you find yourself thinking, 'Apples for only 50p each! What good value!' I heard an interior designer boasting that a florist had hung balls on her Christmas tree for a *mere* £500.

However, expensive areas are great hunting-grounds for charity shop purchases and genteel jumble sales. Rich people throw out extraordinary things.

Grey areas

Really cheap areas also have grey trading shops. That's not a shop chain name, but a description of the way they operate, importing things from cheaper parts of the globe. You will find Colgate toothpaste with Arabic writing on it, unknown brands of biscuit, white tee-shirts....The best shops are like souks.

Look for the sign 'Pound Shop'

Or a name including the word 'pound' in high

streets. In these shops, everything costs a pound. Take care. Leave assumptions behind. I have been caught out in these shops several times. I usually take one of the items on display and proffer my pound. I am sent back like a naughty child; £1 usually buys three of the same items not one, so check quantities.

Cheap hardware, gardening tools and school shirts
There are over two hundred and seventy-five Poundstretcher stores selling eyewateringly cheap hardware, gardening tools and seeds, toys, clothing, trainers... anything but serious food. A typical price quoted to me is a child's white polo shirt, £1.99; unbranded trainers, £6.99.

The store says there's nothing substandard about the quality of what's sold; it's not an outlet for things not good enough to flog at full price elsewhere. They cut their prices by not taking the double-or-more profits that other stores take. You won't find many brand names, though Disney toys and Cadbury and Mars chocolate are on the shelves.

* 0800 1648787 for your nearest store and specific queries.

Ethnic shopping areas are good value
In addition to their intrinsic interest, Bradford's Indian shops sell cheap sacks of rice and nuts, for instance.

Wholesale areas

For general cheapness on everything, you can't rival the Cheetham Hill area of Manchester.

Here within three square miles are all the wholesalers you could dream of, not averse to selling at wholesale prices to you, should they hear what the trade poetically calls 'footfall' in the shop. In London, I like the wholesale area around Spitalfields Market.

Factory shops

Traditional factory shops sold seconds to staff at special prices during breaks. But now factory shops, or that hideous term 'outlets', means any old shop miles from a factory selling things at the same price as anywhere else. However, there are still bargains to be had, as long as you don't spend too much on petrol reaching them. *The Official Great British Factory Shop Guide* has the details.

* £14.99 plus £2 p&p, 34 Park Hill, London, SW4 9PB. 020 7622 3722. Phone for details of shorter regional guides.

Huge and undreamt-of bargains at Government Auctions

A drug-dealer's confiscated motor boat, land and cattle, plant and computers, things lost, stolen, surplus or the sad remains of someone's hopes in the form of their home or business equipment… all of these can be bought at government auction. I read of a washing machine worth £380 sold for £75 and a £2950 Ford van sold for £1700. Perhaps the low prices are because these sales are a bit of a secret; you have to brave a closed shop atmosphere to begin with.

Auction News is a monthly subscription journal carrying details of every sale to be carried out by receivers, county courts, the Ministry of Defence and the Police, grouped by geographical location.

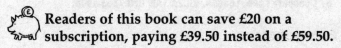 **Readers of this book can save £20 on a subscription, paying £39.50 instead of £59.50.**

* Quote Mr Thrifty Offer, Code 1005, Wentworth Publishing, 17 Fleet Street, London EC4. 0207 353 7300.

Short-notice sales are listed on a dial-a-fax hotline. You call up and press your fax machine's 'receive' button to get a list. 0336 423 488. Calls cost 50p per minute.

The Government Auction Handbook, £14.75, also from Wentworth above, is a good beginners' guide with a full list of auctioneers, how to get on their mailing lists, details on bidding at auction, what to expect, good and bad buys, and lots of enthusiastic encouragement.

Be ahead at auctions
Space limits my mentioning all the auction

houses, but Lots Road, Chelsea is considered best for good finds in furniture. Smaller auction houses will yield treasures. *Auction Insider* is a monthly newsletter for those interested in buying antiques at rather more genteel 'ordinary' auctions (though still cheap). It carries advance auction listings and region-by-region reports on prices achieved for different things sold. Published by Meteor Press, £49.90 for 12 issues.

* 67 Chancery Lane, London, WC2A 1AF. 020 7353 5998.

Buying a reduced-price Rolex or low-cost laptop through Lost Property

If you habitually lose your umbrella, you can replace it cheaply at an auction of lost property. You may have to buy a batch of 20, but if you are absent-minded, you will probably run through them all sooner or later or you can make your purchase pay for itself by selling some on to your friends at a very small profit!

London Transport has a doughty lost property lady called Maureen Beaumont who sends thousands of unclaimed items for sale at 26 sales a year at Greasebys auctioneers.

Sales fall into two brackets. 'Mundane' items (like gloves, wallets, pushchairs) are grouped into bundles of 20. 'Value' things – Rolexes, laptops and musical instruments – go into a higher class of auction which still offers bargains, like an £800 camcorder for £250. There is a small charge for attending the auction. It's not smart. When I went, some bidders hid behind the door, bidding by waving their auction catalogue.

* 211 Longley Road, Tooting, London, SW17 9LG. 020 8672 2972.

A gallimaufry of bargains, news and advice

Supertrader is a new monthly newsletter aimed at small buyers and sellers, from car boot sale weekenders to professionals. It contains tips – what to look for at the annual Perfume Bottle Convention in Bath (a hot venue for collectors, apparently); future collectable hints (save those MacDonald wrappers); people with things like cheap office equipment to sell; Internet bargains and lots more. They are vague about the cost of an annual subscription, saying they are still trying out prices. Make them an offer!

* Fleet Street Publications. 020 7447 4040.

If you have something specific to buy, an admirably comprehensive list of bargain shops, factory outlets, discount warehouses and shopping villages is to be found in *The Good Deal Directory*, published annually each September. If you have specific recommendations, the Directory pays £10 for new traders' addresses.

* £9.99 plus £1 p&p from PO Box 4, Lechlade, Glos., GL7 3YB, or 01367 860016.

Consumer protection by buying with your credit card

Don't run up debts. But paying with a credit card protects your purchases. Depending on the card, you might get 90-day protection against theft or accidental damage and, if you have a dispute with the sellers, some help from the credit card company. If you order something by credit card and it doesn't arrive, you are usually covered by the credit card supplier's insurance.

Check credit card fees regularly. Always choose a card with no annual fee and a six-month low introductory interest rate. But be wary of paying regular subscriptions to anything by card. If you want to cancel the payment, but the payee does not, the credit card company refuses to cancel.

Goldfish Guides

Goldfish Guides are impartial, free guides to buying things from cars to cookers to computers to central heating. They are written along the same lines as *Which?*, the Consumers Association guides, but are smaller and easier to digest and with adverts (which we simply ignore). You can order as many guides as you like. The downside to these is that you receive mail from numerous advertisers, as presumably *Goldfish* makes its money by selling them your details.

* 0870 600 4 600. Website: www.goldfish.com

Advice on what to buy

£59 a year gives you a year's subscription to *Which?* the Consumers Association magazine, providing rigorous buyers' reports on anything you can name.

* 0800 252100.

I am most fond of the Good Housekeeping Institute's consumer reports in the main magazine, and now there is a separate magazine full of them called *GHI Choice*. They also have a free buying advice service; they will personally advise you on what fits your needs.

* 020 7439 5000 for details.

Be an old lady, or keep a pet one

It is a myth that proper workmen rip off the elderly. Keep a frail-looking old lady to 'front' any negotiating you might have with workmen. I was impressed by my mother's ability to get cheap deals from workmen in her old age. Plumbers would waive their fees and leave her free keys to bleed her radiators, builders laid linoleum for her without charge, electricians would charge £5.

Cash and carry

Minimalists need not apply for membership of cash and carry warehouses. These are the places the corner shop buys its stock from, selling huge quantities of anything from cheese to computers. Add the VAT on to the price labels.

To shop at a cash and carry, you sometimes need a business card or VAT number. You may have to apply in advance, or need an introduction from an existing member.

Makro has 27 UK branches selling party-quantities of food and drink by the case, computers (whatever comes in and their own-brand PC at £399) and peripherals (Epson colour inkjet printers, £59), garden equipment and hardware. They prefer you to register in advance to shop here. You (or a friend you can go in with) must be a 'caterer or trader or professional business user'. In practice, that means you're VAT registered, or, if not, self-employed and can show some proof of this, or you have responsibility for ordering things for a business, can show two invoices addressed to you from suppliers, or you can show your name as a director on the bottom of a company's headed paper.

* Application Hotline 0800 450000; headquarters 0161 707 3757.

Personal shoppers

Grand hotels and large department stores often offer personal shopping services. That usually means a woman who will take you shopping or bring things to you in a Personal Shopping Room. 'Tied' shoppers only shop at the department store which employs them, though there is no obligation for you to buy what they suggest. For the most cosseted experience I suggest Harvey Nichols, where you can have a shower, and they may even provide a glass of wine or soft drink and, perhaps food, all for free.

Some personal shoppers call themselves 'wardrobe consultants' who tell you what clothes to throw out or what colours suit you. It can be free, but that person's time must be paid for somehow. So they may take you to the shops which pay them, rather than the shops you need.

If you know what you want, but not where to buy it, the best independent personal shoppers will charge an hourly or half-daily rate to take you on a planned shopping expedition. They can negotiate discounts on your behalf with small shops. If so, you can buy a good quality coat, say, at a considerable discount that pays for your personal shopper and still makes a bargain.

* Shawna Moss has been a personal shopper for twenty years and is the doyenne in the field. She charges a very reasonable £40 an hour, and says she is quick. 09736 38977

The secret wife everyone wants

There is a personal service agency called tenuk for the cash rich and time poor. If you can't afford to wait in for workmen, need someone to shop for birthday presents, book your holiday, deal with a household emergency, want to get a flight upgrade to New York on a Friday night or an appointment with a top hairstylist at 15 minutes' notice, they say they can do it. They will find you reliable workmen and use an army of security-vetted former military guards on scooters who can come to your rescue for any household problem, like being there to receive deliveries. They don't mind how often you use them and you pay extra only when they leave the office on your behalf. It costs £500 plus VAT to join, and although London-based they are expanding so rapidly that by the end of 2000 the service will be nationwide. It's worth asking if they can cover you.

* 020 7563 4200.

Internet bargain basements and bargain-hunting services

There are Internet bargain-hunting services which claim to compare available choices and select the best according to your criteria, either on price or quality or both. Many limit their choices to searching five websites or so, but give it a go.

* Try www.richclickings.co.uk; www.priceoffers.co.uk;
valuemad.com for CDs, software, books, electrics
www.mytaxi.co.uk for a variety of things,
www.empiredirect.co.uk for hi-fis, TVs, electronics
www.abargain.co.uk for anything. Look in any computer
magazine or newspaper computer section for the latest.

Perks from storecards – and you don't even have to buy anything

Most storecard holders are offered 10 per cent
extra off sale prices and a preview day to snap up
the best bargains. All year round, my Harvey
Nichols card gets me cheap parking rates in their
car park in Harriet Street behind the store. If you
don't have a card, show a Harvey Nichols bill for
the sum stipulated at the entrance to get the
parking discount.

* Harvey Nichols, Knightsbridge, London W1, 020 7235 5000.

Getting 10 per cent back on anything

Index (0345 444444) and Argos (0870 600 1010)
are reliably cheap for catalogue shopping and
stores. Buy from one of the traditional mail-order-
only catalogues and you get back a cheque for 10
per cent 'commission' or credit for anything you
buy, including furniture, electronics or carpets.
You get long credit and you can buy house, car
and medical insurance in instalments.
Littlewoods, the second-largest catalogue

company, plans to re-stream its catalogues to have one offering higher prices and credit, and a cheaper one without credit.

* Try Freemans. 0800 731 9731.

Car Boot Sales
Your local paper or *Exchange and Mart* lists nearby sales where ordinary people and small traders sell attic-loads of clothes, toys, antiques and car spares. The *Daily Mail's Weekend* magazine (Saturdays) lists the weekend's best sales and also has other tips. For antiques fairs, which are a cut above car boots, Newark, in Nottinghamshire, is considered the best in Britain.

How to afford fees for schools and universities
It is increasingly hard to make ends meet while you are paying school and university fees. You can improve matters with a little creativity.

Set up a family firm
Other friends dealt with this problem without getting a separation, but by setting up a 'family firm' – a company into which various earnings are put. The children, as shareholders, receive dividends of their tax allowance, £3500 a year, without this going through their parents' income and being declared as tax.

How to sell anything free or very cheap

Most local free papers don't charge for classified advertisements offering things for sale. *Loot* magazine 020 7328 1771 does not charge for advertisements. Save money on the traditional card-in-newsagent, which costs surprisingly high, by filling out a free, provided card at Sainsbury's Homebase and most big supermarkets like Somerfield, which offer a free sales and services board.

If you have something old and interesting, *Homes and Antiques*, and *Period Living* magazine are among those with a free classified advertising section, although you have to wait a few months as the 'lead times' between writing and issuing glossy magazines are long.

Cash Convertors, a national chain of secondhand shops, will buy on the spot *anything* they can test, including CDs. 0207381 6046.

Sell via the local schools

In my area, two enterprising mothers began a free quarterly magazine called the *Interschools Advertiser*. This circulates amongst the local private schools and takes classified advertisements for around £2, with no limit on number of words. It is an excellent way to buy toys, secondhand school uniform and computer equipment, and because they charge higher rates for local businesses to put display ads in its pages, they also make money.

Bartering skills

Brighton has the most organised skill-swop system I know. A directory rates in a currency unit called 'brights' each skill offered by a member, from baking a chocolate cake to lessons in bricklaying. A cake might be two brights, bricklaying, 20. When you use a service, you write a 'cheque' to the other person for the 'price' in brights. They credit this to their bright account, to use against other services in the directory, from any other member. Goodness knows how they balance the accounts, but it works well.

* Bright Exchange can be contacted through Lets Link, the national skill-swop organisation. Quinnell Centre, 2 Kent Street, Portsmouth, Hants, PO1 3BS. 023 9273 0639.

MR THRIFTY GETS THINGS FREE

Take skip luck
Look outside factories and shops in cities, especially in rag trade areas, just after they close. I have found bags of good clothes hangers with designer names on, thread and trimmings.

Again, the more upmarket districts have the best skips, especially theatres and offices that are moving premises. My finds include boxes of discarded fax paper, a papier mâché Greek column from the Royal Opera House (an excellent table) and Christmas tree decorations from an old lady's clearout.

It is illegal to take anything from a skip without the owner's permission, a rule obeyed to the letter by every skip hunter.

Plastic gloves, paper towels
Free from petrol stations, next to the pumps. Useful when washing up and gardening.

Sugar and salt
When buying a cup of tea or coffee, you may feel

like having sugar – and then, stung by the sudden recollection that you want to lose weight, change your mind once you have taken a little packet. When this happens to me, I use it to feed cut flowers at home. Salt can also be collected like this, but don't use it for your flowers!

Matches
From restaurants, hotels and hairdressers.

Postcards
Free in trendy cafés and restaurants, where you usually find postcard holders by the lavatories. You need not eat there to grab a handful, and they are usually stylish and witty.

* For latest places to find cards, try card maker Boomerang, PO Box 7009, Hook, RG27 8YL, or walker@boomerangmedia.co.uk

Rubber bands
If you or neighbours receive lots of post, the postman will drop good thick rubber bands around the front door.

Wrapping paper
Use the paper wrapping from bunches of flowers. Better quality and just as attractive as gift paper at £1 a sheet.

Newspapers

You can read most newspapers each day free at your local library. Of course, you can't then use them to line the cat's tray afterwards. Some big hotel chains have newspapers in the reception areas. A few trendy cafés and burger bars also have them.

Music and brand new books

Big book and record stores have revived the 1950s record shop service of allowing you to listen, through headphones, to free music of your choice for as long as you like, although you may have to stand. Borders bookstore has 600 pre-loaded CDs in its private headphone service; you can also choose virtually any CD from stock and ask to hear it. There is also free live jazz, usually on Friday evenings. Borders book section also lets you select a book and sit reading it for hours if necessary, even over coffee, without having to buy it, although I did see one woman cleaning her nails onto the book whilst doing this.

* For Borders stores, ask at 020 7292 1600.

Free speech and Shakespeare manuscripts

The headphone section of The British Library is the best free attraction in London. You can hear scores of famous voices reading their own work; and you can also see virtually every significant manuscript* in history. There is a free children's book corner and sofas.

*authenticity not guaranteed.

* 96 Euston Road, London NW1. 020 7412 7000.

Free TV heaven

Bradford's National Museum of Photography, Film and Television has five viewing booths (for up to four people each) and a 40-seater viewing theatre which you can book, free, or just turn up on the off-chance. Choose one or all of thousands of recordings of every top TV programme, sit back and enjoy.

* Bradford, BD1 1NQ. Closed Mondays except Bank Holidays; otherwise open 10–6. 01274 202030.

Free information

Internet service Askjeeves.com will answer most queries. Penelope Beaumont tells me that www.bigwig.net//freestuffuk claims to have the best news of anything free.

A free party game for children

Sheets of bubblewrap, from offices or parcels you receive, are the best free party team-game for children. Spread out equal amounts of wrapping and each member of a team in turn, or altogether, has to stamp on it. The first to pop all the bubbles wins.

Free firewood

Don't buy expensive logs. Burn wood from skips or dumps. Chop it into manageable lengths, but *never* burn any wood which has been treated with chemicals, coated or painted.

Free pets

You can acquire these from cat and dog refuges, or try your vet for more odd animals like mice. Be careful what you tell a refuge owner. Some people won't give you a pet, which would love a nice home, if you work full time. It is one thing to ensure an animal has company, walkies or a cat flap, but quite another to be as exacting as I have found some of these people. Tell them you work part time. Square it with your conscience by telling yourself that you do indeed work part time – the part when you're not at home or asleep.

If you want a pedigree but can't afford breeders' prices, ask for a cheaper 'pet standard' animal – those a whisker short of 'show standard'. My beautiful British Blue cat's fur was considered 'too thick and soft' for show.

* The National Pet Register for Lost and Found Pets is at 01423 331233.

MR THRIFTY BUYS A HOUSE AND DOES IT UP

How to buy an interesting house for peanuts

Homesteading is the way to buy a house at about one-third off. This council-run scheme offers houses in need of doing-up at discounts. Ask your local authority Planning Department. Derby City Council even has a Property Sales Centre, 01332 716492.

Also ask the Planning Officer at your local council for a look at the Buildings At Risk register (held by Kent, Essex, Cotswolds, Sheffield and Norfolk, but ask in your area too). Don't be scared of your Planning Officers. Contrary to reputation, some have a deep and practical love of buildings and they might be kind enough to tell you of unloved but interesting buildings in the area.

SAVE is a charity for saving threatened historic buildings, from cottages to follies to factories. Most are listed and unoccupied. Many are not on any estate agent's books, although the owners may be open to offers. 'In many cases,' the leaflet says wisely, 'acquiring the building you've set your heart on may require as much patience and perseverance as the restoration work itself.'

The annual catalogue (150-ish buildings) costs £10 p&p free. See the complete register for £15 via the internet at www.savebritainsheritage.org, where you will also find a free sample. Or phone or write for a free form, and for £5 you can get a printout of the types of property which might interest you, listed by building type and location – England and Wales only.

* Save Britain's Heritage, 70 Cowcross Street, London, EC1M 6EJ. 020 7253 3500. Also try: English Heritage, 020 7973 3000; The Scottish Civic Trust, 0141 221 1466; The Ulster Architectural Heritage Society, 028 9055 0213.

* For tumbledown properties, try Capital Property Lists, which lists anything in need of work. 020 7288 0288.

* Also try home search agents (free directory from the Association of Relocation Agents. 01359 251800).

Dream cottages
In the Sticks magazine has these, plus background information on schools, shops and services in the vicinity of your dream cottage; £27 for 12 issues,.

* Slaggyford, Carlisle, Cumbria, CA6 7NW, 01434 381404/382680. Also www.inthesticks.com

* The National Association of Estate Agents (01926 496800) has a free Homelink service to get details of houses in other areas sent to you.

Repossessed houses

Tragically, cheaper. Check *Exchange & Mart* and similar magazines. *The London Property Guide* lists 2000 places for sale in the South, £29.99 for three months' subscription plus p&p (020 7225 1442). *London Repossession List*, £25 for three issues, 020 8209 0200.

Buying at auction

Local papers might list auctions, and estate agents might help you. You must brave a closed circle of property developers who sometimes batch-buy houses at auction and even view things together. *The London Auction List* gives every vacant property in every residential auction in the area (020 8209 0200) – and if you call the auctioneers, you might learn about other auctions in your area.

House swops

If you can't sell your house, don't want to be stuck in a chain, or want to cut your mortgage by moving to a smaller place and having a lump sum, try exchanging homes. You save estate agents' fees, pay little or no deposit and no stamp duty if you receive under £60,000 in top-up fees to make the exchange equal.

Get your home valued (free) by two estate agents. Take the average price and put a photo of the house in the local paper or newsagent windows in

the area you want to move to, stating what you
seek in return.

If you want to move to a more expensive new
home, most builders will part-exchange on your
house. Barratts have homes for sale nationally,
some new, some bought from others. You must
trade up 20 per cent and pay a registration fee.
Check your local paper for others.

* Barratt Homes, 0191 286811

Avoid paying estate agents' commission
Link-Up Properties charges flat-rate commission
on houses they sell plus £95 registration fee for
six months' marketing. Their commission is £250
including VAT, for properties under £100,000, and
£500 for £100,000 and over. If your property is on
the borderline, they point out thriftily that you
can save £250 by popping your property on the
market at £99,999. There is no commission if they
fail to find you a buyer in eight weeks. The
service is basic: they don't come and value your
home, and you write your own description, buy
their 'For Sale' board (£23.50) and put it up.

How do they sell your house? Through the
national papers, the Internet, a daily paper
mailed to buyers, house-seeking services,
property developers and relocation specialists.

* Link-Up Properties Nationwide Ltd, Sovereign Centre, Victoria Road, Burgess Hill, West Sussex, RH15 9LH. 0800 072 0800.

A fast way to check an area before you move into it

Upmystreet.com will print out all sorts of details about an area, by postcode, including the local rates, popular schools in the area and their league table results, and even the response time should you need to call the Police or an ambulance. Invaluable. HomeSite is a similar service also offering personal printouts especially covering local information on radon gas, subsidence, land use previously and mining. There is £2000 compensation offer if you find them wrong.

* 01722 41188 www.homesight.co.uk

Savings on DIY and gardening things if you've just moved

Great Mills, the DIY superstores, offers a '10 per cent Advantage Discount Card for Homemovers' within six months of your moving home. 01761 416034 for details.

Build it yourself

IKEA has developed a house kit you virtually snap together. Check with them to see if it's arrived here yet. Perhaps you can import it from Sweden, like a car.

Building skills can be easier than they look. A friend replastered her oak-beamed cottage on the same principle as cake-icing, and, 20 years later, it's fine.

When her children were at school and her husband at work, my pal, Penny Butler, built a new house in her back garden. She read manuals and supervised workmen, for whose comfort she bought a cheap caravan as a tea tent. She saved thousands and has a house with enough cupboards. Penny recommends the Association of Self-Builders.

Save loads on building materials

The Association of Self-Builders is a non profit-making club. Members don't have to build a house, merely dream of doing some home improvements. The £25 annual membership gives you access to local groups with all their contacts and ideas and good workmen, a magazine and information sheets. Members get insurance deals and up to 60 per cent discount on building materials from big suppliers like Jewson's and Graham's – the same discounts the big builders get.

* Call Keith Burrell 01604 493757
www.asbbintranets.com
htlp: //www.thisis.co.uk/assoc-selfbuild

Learn building skills in a week

The Association's founder, Simon Clark, also runs weekend or week-long training courses in roofing and rooflights, electrics, insulation, drainage and services, joinery and plumbing and heating at reasonable rates.

* Constructive Individuals, Trinity Pier, 64 Orchard Place, London E14 0JW. 020 7515 9299

DIY materials at a discount

Find a proper builder's supplier in the *Yellow Pages* or similar. Go in once to show your face and make a small purchase, like nails. Return and this time ask for your 20 per cent 'trade loyalty' discount. You won't be asked to prove you're a builder since many workmen don't have a card, and frankly, merchants aren't bothered as long as they shift stock.

Discounted bricks, stone and paving

Sue Gates of Brook Barns is one of the most trustworthy dealers in reclaimed building bricks, stone and wood. She isn't bargain basement, but is meticulous about quality, hand-checks her stone and will always give you a fair price, beginner or builder, buying or selling. For these virtues, you pay before taking away.

* Brook Cottage, Stoney Heath, Ramsdell, Near Basingstoke, Hants., RG26 5SW. 0118 9814379.

In my good books

The Housebuilder's Bible is a one-book, miracle
guide to doing any work on any house. In a
funny and practical way, Mark Brinkley covers
niggles like, 'Is that tree too close to my house?'
(A helpful table specifies each tree type and its
proper distance away). His chapter on 'How to
Double your Building Costs' says that an
ordinary fireplace may cost £200; for an
inglenook, £4000. Handmade floor and wall tiles
add £2300 to the average cost; natural stone adds
£9500 over the cost of a brick house shell.

* £18 including p&p, Rodelia Ltd, PO Box 853, Weston Colville,
Cambridge, CB1 5NZ. 01223 290230.

How to save money on builders

Get all the plumbers, joiners and roofers you
need for emergencies in a year – at one fixed
price. AON Home Assistance is developing a
new insurance policy. You pay an annual
subscription and in an emergency, get access to
any number of workmen, three hours labour and
£100 worth of parts for free.
No limit to the number of call-outs.

* 0800 001310 for details

Get a warranty, not a guarantee, on building work.

Although the Federation of Master Builders has

a complaints procedure, only use a builder registered under the Warranty Scheme, for real protection – including the risk of the builder leaving the job unfinished – and a two-year guarantee. Your builder-member must apply in advance of work and you pay 1 per cent of the contract price. Other insurance-backed guarantees come from the Building Guarantee Scheme (01232 877147) and the National Register of Warranted Builders (020 7404 4155).

Always tell your insurance company if you're having big work done, otherwise if the builder damages your property or himself, they might disallow the claim.

Hiring workmen
The Government-backed Link or CSCS card will show that a person is properly trained. When you brief a workman, remember the difference between an estimate and a quote. An estimate isn't binding; a quote is.

What to ask a workman before giving the go-ahead:
What are your day/hour rates?
Will there be any other mark-ups?
Does that include VAT?
Are you busy?
When might you start?
How long do you think the job will take?

Are you prepared to allow any time over that for possible problems?
Will you be working on this job, or will you send someone else?
How many of you?
What guarantee do you offer?
Are you a member of a trade organisation?

How to get an architect's opinion for £10

RIBA, the architects' association, has around a week each year, usually in Autumn, called 'Architects in the House'. You pay £10 (a donation to Shelter) and they send an architect to your home to give an hour's professional opinion on specific building work you are contemplating, or simply to suggest improvements. It could be Lord Rogers himself!

* 020 7580 5533.

Get in a quantity surveyor or project manager

He will draw up a costing plan with penalty clauses for large projects. Ask local architects for recommendations.

Best free advice

* The Building Centre can give you a shortlist of specialised workpeople in your area, and advice, plus a huge reference library. It's free to visit – but the same information via their phone helpline costs £1.50 a minute. 26 Store Street, London,

WC1E 7BT. 020 7692 4000. Helpline: 09065 161136.

* The Guild of Master Craftsmen recommends members from roofers to mosaic restorers. If things go wrong, use its free impartial conciliatory service. Castle Place, 166 High Street, Lewes, East Sussex, BN7 1XU. 01273 478449.

* Dulux operates an advice centre and an approved decorator service. 01753 550555 for advice; 0845 769 7668 for Trade Select.

* *IDH 2000* is the Interior Designers' Handbook, an industrial-strength address book of suppliers. It costs £75 plus £7.50 plus p&p, from RIBA Bookshop, 66 Portland Place, London W1. 020 72510 7910.

* *Build It* magazine offers a free Ask the Experts Helpline, offering specialist advice on everything from planning regulations to bricklaying and tiling. 020 7865 9042, open 11am–1pm, and 2–4pm.

* *Individual Homes* magazine offers another excellent free helpline. 01527 836600, open Monday to Friday, 9.30am–5pm.

* The Focus Do It All chain of stores has a seven-day DIY helpline open 9am-8pm from Monday to Saturday, and 9am – 6pm on Sundays. 0800 436436.

* *The Building Conservation Directory* is packed with seriously good workpeople and with helpful articles. £19.95 including p&p, Cathedral Communications Ltd, The Tisbury Brewery, Church Street, Tisbury, Wiltshire, SP3 6NH. 01747 871717.

* The Society for the Protection of Ancient Buildings publishes leaflets giving technical advice and organises a two-day 'Introduction to the Repair of Old Buildings', £100, every spring. SPAB is at 37 Spital Square, London, E1 6DY. 020 7377 1644.

* The Georgian Group gives free access by phone to their three architectural historians and also sells booklets on every aspect of interiors and exteriors; £2.75 plus postage. The Group has a fund for restoration grants. 6 Fitzroy Square, London, W1P 6DN. 020 7387 1720.

Mr Thrifty does up his home

National Trust interiors advisor David Mlinaric sensibly told me that if you get the basics of a house right, especially the kitchen and bathroom, considerations like the wall colour are the icing on the cake.

Before you decorate, do your damp course, replaster, get your pipes, roof and heating in order. Put up smoke detectors, extinguishers and a fire blanket for chip fires in the kitchen (they get worse if watered).

Before starting painting, go to a large DIY store and read labels carefully. You can save hours with a metal paint that 'kills' rust as you paint or paint that fills cracks in as you go, or one-coat paint, or fungicidal woodfillers.

Basic once-a-year house maintenance

Before Winter, walk around your outside walls
looking for damp stains, especially where metal,
brick or wood join together, or at corners. Use a
stiff brush to clear the damp-course at the foot of
the walls and gutters and put wire netting over
the top to stop leaves gathering.

Watermarks under the windows mean the groove
under the sill is blocked. Chisel out a new
channel for drips if necessary and check that the
sills are properly painted underneath to stop rot.
You might consider sealing your house front with
a water sealant paint, a see-through matt coating
which protects against fungus, frost and damp,
and reduces heat loss from inside.

Plumbing

For blocked sinks and lavatories, use a plunger
from any hardware store or unpick a wire
coathanger and poke it down the U-bend. Before
calling a plumber, buy caustic soda from a
hardware shop which may burn the blockage
away. A plumber's tip is One-Stop Drain Cleaner
from hardware shops, who may refuse officiously
to hand it over saying 'It's only for trade'. Reply,
'My plumber said it's for everyone'.

Decorating at a discount

Take any wallpaper or fabric outside the shop

before buying. The shop lights will drain the colour and it won't look the same at home. Take a swatch home; your light there will be quite different.

If you have fallen for some fabric, but it's too expensive or the wrong colour, contact the maker direct. If you want a reasonable amount – say 20 metres – they will help. I once phoned a maker whose design was printed on thin silk and asked if there was a cheaper option. 'No problem; I'll print it on cotton for you,' she replied. 'I've printed on sacking.'

For really big amounts, you should get a discount anyway. I ordered 70 metres of cheap velvet and ended up with a reduction of several pounds a metre to £3.95 a metre and, of course, free delivery.

* Just Fabrics, 01566 776279 has one of the largest sample stocks in the country and can offer anything on a discount. There is also a research service.

The Curtain Exchange stocks designers' mistakes and secondhand curtains of every style, and will advise, measure, make and hang new curtains. You can take curtains home for a 24-hour test before you buy. Or trade in your old curtains for 50–60 per cent of the resale value.

* 01376 561199 for branches round the country.

Cheap sales of antique linen and lace

Patricia Hovey tells me she does a lot of rather lovely ironing for her local Oxfam shop. It specialises in monthly sales of antique linen and lace: old sheets, tablecloths, pillowcases and clothes which stand the test of time, for a fraction of the cost of a new, less substantial purchase. Write to Mrs Hovey enclosing an SAE for more information on forthcoming sales.

* Oxfam Shop, 46 Highgate, Kendal, Cumbria, LA9 4TF.

Buy furniture at auction

You can pay anything from £5. Lucinda Lambton furnished her Gothic rectory with pieces they all-but paid her to cart away in Liverpool. Lots Road Auction Galleries, 71 Lots Road, London, SW10 0RN, 020 7351 7771, hold viewings each weekend. The 'car boot' market on Sunday mornings next to Brighton station is a treasure trove, too.

To go in for antiques spotting in a serious way, buy any *Miller's Guide*.

For one-offs

Get a craftsman-maker to make you something. It won't cost any more than buying it from a shop and you'll get something made to fit. Consult the Crafts Council, 020 7278 7700, whose library has

photos of hundreds of members' work (44a
Pentonville Road, London N1 9BY). Hooke Park
College in Dorset is full of dedicated furniture
designer-makers. Go to an end-of-year show here
or at any art college and see what you can find.
01308 863 130.

Floorcoverings
The cheapest way to smarten a floor is to lay down
chipboard and spray-paint with car paints. Do the
corners first and back your way towards the door or
you will be marooned! I have done this successfully
in my kitchen and it gets lots of admiration.

Curtain poles
Can cost hundreds in decorating shops, but about
£10 (if that) from proper wood suppliers or DIY
wood shops if you buy thick dowelling meant for
banisters and paint or stain it. You can buy cheap
curtain hooks and finials from DIY or fabric shops
or make your own by painting a cheap wooden
doorhandle at each end.

Furniture
Garden furniture is a cheap substitute until you can
afford the 'real' thing. It is worth buying antique
furniture if it suits you, because you can always
resell it, either to the same dealer or another one, at
a profit.

Ideas for interiors

A new service from smart designers is www.interiorinternet.com, offering things from 'one impartial source with a design conscience,' whatever you make of that. Names like Andrew Martin and Nicholas Haslam have put unique things for sale on the site. You can enter the kind of things a person wants and the site will offer gift suggestions; you can gather matching products together to store for a new room or house before buying; you can produce an image of your room to see what the thing looks like in it; and you can call them personally too. Shoppers are given a Virtual Store Card; the higher your spend, the better percentage discount you are given for future shopping.

Shop fittings can be fun. Used lockers and metal shelves are particularly cheap. Try Midland Steel Equipment, King Street, Creswell, Near Worksop, Notts, S80 4ER. 01909 721090 for a free brochure.

Architectural salvage is my way of life. These warehouses and yards are bliss for rummagers and sell sofas, cinema seating, baths, garden statues, light fittings, old wood for floors... everything. I once spent £40 on a washstand with bowl (referred to as a French tart's), then had it re-enamelled and installed, and saw the same thing for £2000 in a shop. Cut bath re-enamelling costs by going to motorbike repair shops, who are cheaper than garages and know about spraying metal.

Make your own

Make bookcases of planks supported by bricks. Wooden pallets, bakers' delivery crates or plastic milk crates make excellent bed bases. Car seats from breakers' yards make easy chairs. You can make a round circular table from a round cable drum, covered with a cloth.

Use polystyrene pellets used to pack hi-fis (beg them in quantity from electrical shops), fill a dustbin bag, and hey presto! Sag bag seating.

For lampshades, use a domed muslin food cover from hardware stores or an upside-down-wicker fruit basket.

Cutting house insurance costs

Get an independent broker to phone around, or call the main companies yourself.

For insurance, pay in instalments. Direct Line offers monthly instalments at no extra cost for home and car insurance. There are knock-on benefits. If you take out their comprehensive car insurance, you save 50 per cent on their rescue

service, run by the admirable Europ Assistance.
020 8253 8118.

Others who offer instalments include: CGU
Direct (0800 121 004), Norwich Union Direct
(0800 888 222 – home insurance and
PremiumSearch (0800 109876).

You can get cheaper house insurance if you fit
window locks, a burglar alarm and if you say
that, when you go away, you will have a
professional homesitter (from the small ad pages
of smart house magazines) or someone else there.

Animal Friends is a new non profit-making
insurance company set up by two animal-loving
former lawyers to fund the big animal charities
by donating 10-20 per cent of the premium you
pay. It offers house, motor, travel and business
insurance underwritten by Lloyds of London.

* 0870 444 3438, www.animalfriends.org.uk

Fitting a burglar alarm
There are a huge number of cowboys in this field,
and as many burglar alarms left to ring
unattended. You could purchase an empty box
that looks like a burglar alarm. My friendly
detective tells me that the Police need colour
video surveillance to identify anyone to court-
proof standards.

Everything's lovely in Mr Thrifty's garden

Keep your weeds down by lining the flower-beds with a plastic dustbin liner with holes cut in it for those plants you want to grow. Disguise the plastic with earth or gravel on top.

Free and cheap plants

Seeds are 20 times cheaper than the same variety bought as a plant. The Suttons Seeds catalogue is free. Not the cheapest, but good quality and comprehensive.

* Suttons Seeds Ltd, Woodview Road, Paignton, Devon, TQ4 7NG. 01803 696300.

'Harvest' free seeds from existing flowers. Keep the dried heads, turn upside down and shake into a plastic bag. The seeds will come out. Joining the Heritage Seed Programme gives you access to a free seed library of rare or endangered species. It costs £18, or £9 for members of the Association (around £18.50 with concessions for young or old). Members also get six free seed packets a year and access to a free advice line, gardens and free booklets on organic vegetable growing.

* Henry Doubleday Research Association, Ryton-on-Dunsmore, Coventry, SV8 3LG. 024 7630 3517.

Another good way to get free plants is to become

friendly with your local park-keeper. S/he will often have bulbs or even plants not wanted next season to give away.

Gardeners are usually happy to give you cuttings of anything you admire, though not at formal gardens like Sissinghurst, where they're swamped with requests. To propagate easy things like geraniums, pop a cutting in water until you see roots, then plant. But it's better to use a hormone rooting powder as a growing aid, like Murphy's, which contains fungicide, costs around £1.50 and lasts a year. Don't buy gel rooting mediums; roots can get stuck in them.

Cheap garden basics

You can make enormous savings on everyday gardening basics like fertiliser by joining an Allotment Society as a Garden Member for a few pounds. Go to the Hut on your nearest allotments, which you will usually find open on Saturday and Sunday mornings between 9.30 and 11.30. You must join before you buy. Then you can buy things like fish blood and bone for around half the price it costs in garden centres – usually cost price and about 10p extra for bags and general hut maintenance.

Zero-maintenance hanging baskets

Drivers' heads swivel when they sit at traffic

lights admiring the hanging baskets of Bloxhams in Beckenham, Kent. No flower shop ever sold such luxuriant blossoms, never wilted or brown. On investigation, Mr Thrifty discovered they are actually cunning imitation plants. At £40-ish, they cost more than the real, growing McCoy, but need no maintenance, and last several years. The florist remarked, if you want to make your neighbours see green, spray the imitation baskets with water every once in a while.

* 020 8466 0508 for details.

MR THRIFTY'S LARDER

Supermarkets

Avoid supermarkets. I am told that the average visit costs £6 in overheads, like parking and cups of coffee, not to mention the temptation to buy treats which can increase your bill by up to 40 per cent – the average figure for impulse buys. If you shop locally instead, the food may not be cheaper but there's less to buy and you can't pile a trolley to skyscraper level. I have halved my food bills and still eaten well by doing this.

There are social benefits to local shopping, too. You support your local small shops. And you never know what will happen. I once loudly urged everyone in a greengrocer to buy British apples and the greengrocer gave me a big bag of free apples. British ones.

The never never: rules of engagement when supermarket shopping.

Never shop when hungry. You will buy more.

Never visit a supermarket before lunch time. After

lunch, they begin reducing perishable things like steak, cream and fancy bread. Arrive just before they close and you'll speed down the aisles with all the best bargains.

Never assume larger 'economy packs' of anything are cheaper. I once heard a soap company executive chortling that this was not the case with soap powder.

And *never* believe that things on the 'bargain' section are bargains without checking. Supermarkets cheekily use these shelves to offload things they want to clear quickly.

Economy ranges

Their consciences pricked by their profits, supermarkets' Economy, Basic or whatsitsname ranges are tremendous value. You must be careful, though. Baked beans for 9p are all very well, but 21p washing up liquid is so watery that you need to tip most of the bottle in to get a result.

Own brands

Some makers, like Kellogg's, won't make food for supermarkets. But if makers do rip-off their own products for supermarket own brands, they will normally be made to lower standards. Biscuits will contain fewer chocolate chips, or whatever. I've heard manufacturers privately crow about how they do this, but complain that M&S Foods are more exacting than their own standards people. Another brand which is made to exceptionally high standards is Co-op; hard taskmasters to wholesalers as they demand top purity standards and ethical behaviour from their suppliers.

* Sainsbury's gives you a penny for every carrier bag you bring with you.

Put fruit and vegetables in bags yourself

If I spend £2.50 in a greengrocer, I leave the shop laden. The same sum in a supermarket fresh produce section goes virtually nowhere. Supermarkets have subtle ways of increasing your spending on ordinary things, for instance, by wrapping fruit and vegetables in cellophane to make it look superior, cleaner, 'selected' (was the other kind not chosen by someone?) or 'ready-prepared'. The trade call this 'premium' produce, in other words, they charge more for it. You still have to wash everything before cooking it, and peel potatoes, no matter how little dirt they have on them, so it's not worth paying extra. Street markets are dirt-cheap without being dirtier.

Loyalty cards

Supermarkets and chain stores make much of their loyalty card schemes, which give you points on your bill, which add up to money off the next bill. The Consumers' Association says the average family saves £26 a year with these cards. Tesco has a labyrinthine scheme with extra 'keys' for discounts on other things like flights and theatre tickets. My feeling is: use these cards when they're easy, but life is too short to collect the set. Anyway, you'll break valuable wallet leather squeezing all that plastic in.

Boots' Advantage card comes out well, giving four points per pound spent, although these can only be spent on 'selected items' in the store. Barclaycard Profile points get my booby prize for the most lacklustre selection of rewards.

Food sold from its cardboard boxes

Aldi and Netto are pile 'em high sell 'em cheap names to look out for, in addition to good old Kwiksave. They're not plush. You won't find the helpful, leisurely interest which Waitrose staff show their customers. Grab a cardboard box, pile in with your purchases and go. Lidl sells more than food: cheap jeans, garden equipment and electronics can be found.

* 0870 6081315.

Costco is a different animal, a membership warehouse shopping club. To join you must have an ID card, such as those issued by hospitals to

staff. Food is around 20 per cent cheaper than
shops; clothes, like Armani jeans, Yves St Laurent
shirts or Sony electricals, are up to 26 per cent
cheaper. Food comes in larger catering packs, and
tins come in sixes or twenty-fours.

* 01923 213113 for information, Monday to Friday.

Buy direct from growers and farmers
In certain areas, especially the East of England,
I stop at houses displaying For Sale signs to buy
fresh-laid eggs and home-grown vegetables, jams,
pot plants and flowers from their gardens very
cheaply. This is part of our country way of life.
I feel sure that some health inspector will one day
try to stamp it out, so enjoy it while you can.

Farmers' Markets are a way for small local food
producers to sell direct, mainly fruit and veg but
often meat, cheese and seasonal things like
Christmas trees. They are not to be confused with
fairs at which a miserable bunch of foodies sell
loaves for £2.50, nor are they joyous street markets
where silver-tongued orators proclaim,
'I won't ask you to pay £10... I won't ask £5....'

Held weekly in increasing numbers of towns and
cities like Arundel, Bath, Bridport, Bristol,
Cullompton, Frome, Gloucester, Halifax, Holm,
Lewes, Newbury, Stratford-on-Avon and
Tunbridge Wells; prices are low because you're

saving the cost of transport elsewhere and shop overheads.

* For more details, call your Council's Local Agenda 21 Officer or Economic Development section, or send an SAE marked 'Farmers' Markets' to: The Soil Association, Bristol House, 40–56 Victoria Street, Bristol, BS1 6BY.

Pick your own

Fruit and vegetables are pounds cheaper than in supermarkets if you pick your own, and pick-your-own farmers try to offer free fun like tractor trips while you're there. Send two first class stamps for details of farm shops and pick-your-own farms in your area.

* Farm Retail Association, The Greenhouse, PO Box 575, Southampton, SO15 7ZB.

Grow your own mushrooms

Ann Miller bought a mushroom-growing kit from a garden centre and it failed. So she experimented – finding that you can grow mushrooms a treat on toilet rolls – and now runs her own mushroom-kit business. Her £3 kits give you exotic fresh mushrooms at a fraction of the cost of shop-bought varieties. Ann's 'ready to crop' logs of around half a metre long will continue producing for three years. She also sells wooden dowels impregnated with mushroom spores which you pop into your own logs – though you wait a year for them to grow. For patient gourmets, there's a truffle-growing kit which will take six years to crop.

* Send a large SAE for her catalogue to Ann Miller's Speciality Mushrooms, Greenbank, Melkie Wartie, Inverurie, Aberdeenshire, AB51 5AA.

Buying from wholesale markets
If you have many mouths to feed, a large freezer or are giving a party, it is worth getting up early to go to your nearest wholesale market for meat, fish, fruit and vegetables. Outside London, officially it's 'trade only', but as one seller confided, 'We're not going to refuse anyone who comes with money in their pocket'. You don't have to buy vast quantities. If you're shy, pretend to be shopping for a corner shop or co-operative.

Before setting out, check opening times and any limitations – for example, some markets get shirty if you take a car inside.

* For your nearest wholesale market, consult your local council or try the *Fresh Produce Consortium's Handbook*, £25, from 266–270 Flower Market, New Covent Garden, London, SW8 5NB 020 7627 3391. Order from the library.

Savings on fruit, vegetables and flowers

New Covent Garden fruit and vegetable market runs from 4 to 11am on weekdays and from 9am on Saturdays. Go early for bargains. It is free if you are on foot, bicycle or motorcycle, otherwise parking costs £3.

Most buyers might let you have a few oranges or a bunch of flowers, but some insist that you buy by the box. High street florists mark up their flowers by as much as 300 per cent so you can imagine the savings to be made on flowers here, especially if you are having a party or giving a wedding reception. You won't get huge savings unless you buy in bulk, but you will always get better-quality, fresher produce. The flower market sells excellent sundries, like ribbons, wire and Oasis arranging foam.

* Nine Elms, Battersea, London, SW8 5NX. 020 7720 2211.

Getting food delivered

Food deliveries are the way of the future. They were the way of the past, when an army of delivery boys took to the streets on capaciously-basketed bicycles. To my mind, any shop which delivers is saving your time and money spent on taking the car out. If a supermarket delivers in your area, expect to be charged up to £5, and don't expect delivery for several days sometimes. There may be a minimum spend before they will deliver, too. Iceland is outstanding, with free deliveries by helpful people who carry things upstairs.

The Fresh Food Company is a well-established company offering a catalogue of organic and environmentally-friendly food, including vegetables, fruit, meat and fish, which you order by 11am on Tuesday to be delivered the following Thursday. Reliable and good at personal service.

 Reader's of this book can claim 10% off the first order over £15, until the end of 2001. Quote 'Mr Thrifty' to get this. One per household.

* 326 Portobello Road, London, W10 5RU. 020 8969 0351. Their Internet ordering site is www.freshfood.co.uk, which they say has a special 'talk to me' button on it.

Buying meat

For bulk meat buys, contact a local meat wholesaler through *Yellow Pages* and ask for a discount. If you want to buy at really good prices, there are three early morning meat markets: London, Liverpool and Glasgow. Smithfield is happy to sell to non-trade customers and opens from 4 to 10am on weekdays. You won't find beautifully-prepared cuts, but you can buy sausages and birds for one-off meals. There's also Central Markets, off Farringdon Road, London,

EC1A 9LH. Liverpool Stanley Market, Edge Lane, Liverpool, L13 2LT, opens weekdays from 4 to 11am. Duke Street Market, Glasgow, opens from 5am to 3pm.

Restaurants' secret butchers
If you need a lot of ready-prepared cuts, or skilful stuff like crown of lamb, catering butchers are the secret of restaurants and professional caterers. Contact a local one through the National Association of Catering Butchers.

* c/o FCI Ltd., Top floor, Salford House, New Street, Stourport-on-Severn, Worcs. DY13 8UE. 01299 822555.

Buying fish
Any real wet fishmonger will fillet a fish free for you. Billingsgate, London E14, is open to the public from 5 to 8.30 am Tuesday to Saturday, selling at wholesale prices. You may find other wholesale fish markets in your region.

If you live within striking distance of a port, local fishing boats will be delighted to sell you their catch cheaply as they unload. Newlyn, near Penzance in Cornwall, has a flourishing fish market which opens at 8am daily. The Newlyn Fish Company, however, opens an hour earlier, selling fresh, frozen and smoked fish at wholesale prices until 4pm on weekdays and midday on

Saturdays. They say that Mr Thrifty readers can ignore the sign directed at the hoi polloi stating 'open from 10am' and walk right in.

* Unit 15, Stable Hobba, The Coombe, Newlyn, Cornwall. 01736 369814.

Cheap nibbles

Julian Graves is an excellent chain of around sixty shops specialising in huge bags of nuts, shelled and natural, dried fruit, nibbles like yoghurt-and chocolate-coated nuts, muesli, porridge oats, spices and the odd strange find like banana-smelling candles, at prices more from souk than supermarket.

 10% discount on presentation of this book

* For shop addresses or a mail-order catalogue, call 01384 277772.

Cheap chocs including champagne truffles

Maxwell & Kennedy, makers of fine chocolates, sell bags of broken champagne truffles and other goodies, at affordable prices. Worth looking out for, but no mail order as this is a casual shop-by-shop deal.

* For your nearest branch, call 020 7491 0939 but don't say you're calling about the cheap chocolates as they are rather touchy on the subject.

Cadbury World

You need not actually visit the tourist attraction here (though you would miss out on fun and free chocolate if you don't). You can pop quietly into the shop for cut-price chocolate misshapes and bargains. While there, feast your eyes on the free 'ordinary' museum at the back of the main attraction with its grand old chocolate boxes and sepia photos.

* Linden Road, Bournville, Birmingham,
BL30 2LD. 0121 451 4180.

How to get a professional chef to cook your dinner party

Phone a local restaurant and ask them to cook you a takeaway. Pride in the job leads them to add in loads of free extras, like dressed salads. I used a local restaurant to cook me my favourite meal, Lamb in Hay, when I was tied up all morning but had guests for lunch. They agreed, at a price that would hardly cover their gas bill, but I had to provide the meat. I scoured Sainsbury's in my dressing gown, for a lamb joint.

Money off drinks

With duty on wine at £1 a bottle, bargain-hunters should cross the Channel to get the same wine cheaper in the shopping areas of Calais. Tesco's champagne here costs a good few pounds less than the same bottles bought here.

In Britain, most off-licences and supermarket wine sellers offer 10 per cent off wines if you buy six bottles at a time. Ask for a free cardboard carrier to take them away. Local Oddbins will deliver free.

Free wine

You can taste a selection of fine wines, educating your palate for free, by haunting the free tastings which precede fine wine auctions. For times and dates, apply for catalogues or ask auction houses, or see the back pages of *Decanter*, the wine magazine sold by off licences.

* Sothebys, 020 7293 6423; Christies, 020 7389 2740.

If you want to taste wines nearer home, off-licence chains have tastings most weekends. Oddbins has free tastings of wine, beer and whisky during quiet times like Sundays which your local manager will tip you off about (020 8944 4400 or www.oddbins.co.uk for local branches), whilst Unwins offers occasional Saturday afternoons (01322 272711 for details).

Majestic wine warehouses offer up to ten wines to taste free at their wine-tasting counters open during normal hours, and also what they call 'major tasting weekends' concentrating on particular types of wine. If you like something, you must buy a case of twelve, but they point out that you can mix these and they offer drinks by small, cheap producers you can't find elsewhere.

* 01923 298200. www.majestic.co.uk

Victoria Wine has monthly tastings of wine and other drinks.

* 01483 715066 for details.

Wine online

ChateauOnline.co.uk offers delivery and 800 wines picked and recommended by the former Sommelier at the Paris Ritz, at 'value' prices for a minimum of six bottles. I tested it by investigating champagne. It could not provide many well-known names, but convincingly, without tasting, sold small producers to me, at very reasonable prices. Sadly, the order-taking part of the site repeatedly collapsed, and that was that. See for yourself.

My favourite vintner

Desert Island Wines is a small, personal mail-order service run from the cellars of eccentric Devon hotel Huntsham Court, by generous-hearted owner, Mogens Bolwig, who globetrots to buy his stock. Wines are randomly reduced, often to ridiculous prices, according to the patron's

mood, and his recommendations turn out to be
perfect.

* 01398 361 365.

Make your own beer, wine and soft drinks
Use kits from major branches of Boots. You can also
make non-alcoholic drinks like ginger beer,
dandelion and burdock, and elderflower
champagne.

10 per cent off tea and coffee
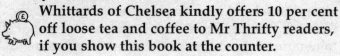 **Whittards of Chelsea kindly offers 10 per cent
off loose tea and coffee to Mr Thrifty readers,
if you show this book at the counter.**

* 0800 525092 for nationwide branches.

Free samples
H.R. Higgins (Coffee-Man) Ltd gives free 100g
samples with orders over 2.5kg for tea and coffee.

* 79 Duke Street, London, W1M 6AS. 020 7629 3913.

The White House of Nottingham operates the most
generous sample-giving system. The catalogue of
teas and coffees comes with a free 100g of good
coffee beans (you can get tea, including herbal, if
you ask). If you order 500g, you get a 10 per cent

discount. There is a rather hefty postage charge, £4.56, but you can make a joint order with friends and split that.

 Mention Mr Thrifty and you will be entitled to free carriage on your first order.

* 0115 9419033.

Cutting down on waste

Don't waste money on plastic containers dedicated to storing food. A bowl, covered by a saucer, costs nothing. Some more robustly constructed margarine containers, like Vitalite's, last years and have a clip-on lid. If you freeze food, don't invest in special labels or pens. Ballpoint on the original paper label is fine.

Don't waste milk. Have a family agreement that the nearest bottle at the front of the fridge door is always used first, and the newest milk goes at the back, or mark the tops with the days of the week.

In extremis

Eat vegetable soup. Even old vegetables can go into this – just cut off any grim-looking bits, peel, check the rest is wholesome and chuck in. Use economy bags of carrots, onions and anything else you have, with potatoes, beans, rice or pasta to thicken. Add water, boil and liquidise. For luxury, add milk and pepper and perhaps a dash of orange juice. One pan will fill you for days, with toast made from supermarket economy bread at around 11p a loaf – choose 'thin sliced' and you get extra slices for your bread.

Saving money on flowers

'A superior bunch of a dozen red roses for £6, wrapped.' Aristocratic flower shop Moyses Stevens offers this bargain to personal callers only. It's a no-frills deal, but is considerably better than bunches you buy from roadside sellers which wilt when you get them home. You also get Moyses' posh paper wrapping, making them look a vastly more extravagant purchase.

* 157 Sloane Street, London SW1. 020 7259 9303.

Making your flowers last longer

Always cut the ends of flowers, with a deep groove up the stem. Then add a few spoonfuls of sugar, lemonade or other sugary substance.

The reason behind the popularity of the much-derided but pretty carnation and chrysanthemum is that they last longest in vases, up to two weeks in sugar water. For house vases, don't buy over priced greenery from the florist but add something from the garden.

Don't order flowers by phone

You can't see what you're sending – and some florists use the opportunity to send half-dying old stock. On the phone, florists try to nudge up their prices, saying something like, 'If you want anything worth sending, you need £20'. But if you went in person into their shop and chose £10-worth of flowers, you would have both hands full. Try to personally oversee them arranging the bouquet and spend the saving on a minicab taking the flowers to their recipient.

I never use networks like Teleflorist or Interflora. If their members need to phone your order to another part of the country, they charge you pounds extra. Save the money by calling *Talking Pages* (0800 600900) for a florist near the recipient of your flowers, then phone your order direct to them, incurring only their local delivery charge of a few pounds.

A good tip is Forever Flowering, with fresh flowers delivered next day anywhere in the UK for £25 and around £7.50 delivery; however, Mr Thrifty sends their dried lavender and roses – £15 a bunch, lasts for ever.

* **020 8392 9929.**

MR THRIFTY ENTERTAINS HIMSELF

The best method of saving money is to stay at home, out of the way of temptation to spend money and where no parking meter can fix you with a glittering eye and urge you to pump money into it.

The radio is free. The Internet claims to be a source of downloading free music; in practice I have found it impossible to get without investing in arcane software.

Hiring videos leaves you open to forgetting to return them and incurring huge fines. Better to record from the television if you can master your video recorder. Choices Direct can sell you PVCs, or pre-viewed videos – of all kinds – at a reduced rate of £4.50, and has a huge and wonderful choice of new videos and audio speaking tapes, DVDs and CDs. Call and ask if you can't find what you want. There are free videos if you tot up enough loyalty points.

* PO Box 190, Peterborough, PE2 6UW. 01733 232800; orders@choicesdirect.co.uk; www.choicesdirect.co.uk

Should you feel the need to go to the cinema, rather than hire a video cheaply, take your own refreshments rather than paying £2 for an ice lolly.

Free tickets to shows

Tickets to recordings of television and radio programmes are free. Ask at your local station.

The BBC has an organised system. Call their Audience Services to talk to a real person from Monday to Friday, 9am–6pm. You can also hear a recorded list of upcoming shows and book by push button phone if you prefer. In the case of television, try to book 12 weeks in advance; but a week beforehand, or even on the day, you can usually get radio tickets and also returned tickets for television.

* BBC Audience Services, 020 8576 1227. Save your phone bill by faxing your request: 020 8576 8802. Or see what is available over the internet: www.bbc.co.uk/tickets/ and e-mail your request following the website's instructions. Also at Pebble Mill Studios, Birmingham, 0121 432 8888.

Half-price theatre tickets

You can buy half-price good seats for top London shows on the day, from 'Les Misérables' to the Royal Shakespeare Company, at the Half-Price Ticket Booth, The Clocktower Building, Leicester Square.

Apparently, other theatre ticket-sellers in the vicinity claim to be 'official' half-price ticket sellers and are nothing of the kind, so find the original building in the centre of the square, looking rather like a lavatory. It is open from Monday to Saturday, 12am-6.30pm and on Sunday from 12am to 3pm. You pay cash only, plus a £2 booking fee, and you get the best available seats.

Discounted theatre tickets for adults and free theatre tickets for children

The Society of London Theatres publishes a free Theatreland supplement which lists discounts available for groups going to the theatre. It also runs Kids' Week in the West End during the last week of the school summer holidays. All children can see a show free, accompanied by a fully paying adult. Other free events will make this worthwhile, like giveaways in the foyer, for instance.

* Put yourself on the priority mailing list for Theatreland supplements or Kids' Week by phoning 020 7557 6700, or look up the website: www.officiallondontheatre.co.uk

Free days out at National Trust houses

Every National Trust property has a free day each year. You don't have to pay to get in. End of story. Call the attraction of your choice and find out its day – which may be sometime in September.

A card giving you free access to 17 London museums, galleries and exhibitions

Now that many museums rightly offer free entry for children, discount season ticket-type arrangements are less good value for families. But if you are an adult and like to gad around museums and exhibitions, £16 buys you a three-day GoSee card allowing free entry to lots of attractions. This makes sense if, say, you visit the Natural History Museum (normally £6.50), the Imax Cinema (£6.50) and the London Transport Museum (£5.50). £26 gives you a free week; £32 is the family three-day pass (two adults, four children); and £50 the family seven-day rate. Originally for foreign tourists, this is now available to all.

* 020 7923 0807

Free admission to over 200 museums, galleries and historic houses

The National Art Collections Fund is the largest charity dishing out dosh to our public art collections. An annual subscription gives you free entry to lots of galleries, museums and historic houses throughout the country, like Kensington Palace. You also get discounted entry to special exhibitions at the Royal Academy, National Galleries of Scotland and Tate Galleries in London and Liverpool.

They send you a prestigious coffee-table-type quarterly magazine, *Art Quarterly*, and a huge annual catalogue of new acquisitions too. Subscriptions are £18 for under-25s and over-60s, £26 for a double special rate, then £27 ordinary single, £40 double and £45 family with up to 6 children.

* **The National Art Collections Fund, Millais House, 7 Cromwell Place, London, SW7 2JN. 020 7225 4800.**

Books on tape for £2.99

The Tape Exchange Mail Order Scheme was set up by Lord Gerald Fitzalan-Howard because, he says, 'spoken word cassettes are expensive and only last two or three hours, and you may only want to hear them once'.

You buy your first tape from the Exchange's huge list for £9.99. Keep it in reasonable quality, and you can swop it for another one for £2.99 at any Welcome Break service station, or by mail order. You can do this as often as you like. More places where you can stop and swop will be added. If your swopped tape is faulty, just return it for a refund or replacement.

* **Carlton Towers, Goole, Yorkshire, DN14 9LZ. 01405 861951.**

Stay in and read a book

Reading saves money on electricity used for TVs

and radios. Nor do you need expensive software on a computer.

Shops claiming to offer discounts simply waste your time if the selection consists of badly-printed picture books.

Postscript offers publishers' remainders – in effect, end-of-season sale books – at half the published price or less, by mail order only. It publishes 10 free catalogues a year covering history, military matters, biography, travel, gardening, cookery and literature. It's not a book club; there's no obligation to order anything.

* 24 Langroyd Road, London, SW17 7PL. 020 8767 7421.

For discounted new books
Check Borders bookshops, amazon.co.uk and www.amazon.com.

Bibliophile Books offers remainders at under half-price to personal callers (9am–4.30pm, Monday to Friday) or by mail order from a newspaper-like catalogue, listing three thousand books under these headings: fiction, biography, war and militaria, erotica, entertainment, crosswords/dictionaries, children's, music. Postage costs a flat rate of £3 per order.

* Unit 5, Thomas Road, London, E14 7BN. 020 7515 9222.

The biggest secondhand bookshop

Hay-on-Wye is Britain's secondhand book capital. Here, Richard Booth reigns (he declared himself King of Hay some years ago) over millions of miles of books on every subject. Hay Castle is for fine and specialist books including art; 44 Lion Street, Hay-on-Wye, Herefordsire, HR3 5SQ for everything else. You can use the net or, they suggest, why not ring and ask if they have the book?

* 01497 820503. www.richardbooth.demon.co.uk, or e-mail castle@richardbooth.demon.co.uk

Order it from the library

There's no need to buy books from bookshops. Public libraries now sell off the better old books at around 30–50p each because of a pressing need, it seems, to make room for more tapes and Catherine Cookson books.

If you can't find something interesting for sale, order newly-published titles from the library at a charge of around 75p. If they don't have it, they will jolly well have to buy it. Determined book-ordering counteracts the trend in libraries to stock up with trivia. It also saves you the cost of constructing expensive bookshelves at home to hold books you will never read twice.

Private libraries

As an alternative to increasingly scruffy and underfunded public libraries, think about joining a private lending library. These are often in beautiful, historic places all over Britain and you pay an annual subscription of from £15 to £150, depending on the place.

The London Library, for instance, has over a million books, strong on new fiction, history, biography and old periodicals. The individual subscription is £150 per year, a good bargain if you read or research a lot and would otherwise need to buy books.

Its central London building is quiet, scholarly and a great place to peruse every possible periodical and newspaper each day for free. I think of it as akin to having an eccentric, generous and excessively bookish uncle who is willing to lend up to 10 volumes, sometimes old and beautiful books which you could never find except in grand collections, and would never normally be loaned. Taking-out times are in months rather than weeks, unlike tedious public libraries. There are no overdue fines.

If you live 'in the country' you can take out 15 volumes and operate everything by post, or phone up, getting staff to locate your books and post them for the cost of the postage.

I have found the staff extremely helpful whatever my request, including locating books they don't have and telling me of other libraries which have them. They can actually get you such books too, saving you telephone tediousness and shoe leather, but at a cost.

* 14 St James's Square, London, SW1Y 4LG. 020 7766 4720. Non-members can browse the computerised catalogue showing many, but not all, books on http://www.londonlibrary.co.uk

A private club for around £100 and a good lunch for £10

Private clubs often cost upwards of several hundred pounds to join. Manchester's Portico Library offers members (known as proprietors) its stock of nineteenth-century books plus rather good lunches at around £10 for three courses. It doesn't serve wine but you can bring your own bottle and some proprietors keep a small private cellar for their exclusive use. There are also musical and other social evenings. A spectrum of ages, sexes and types of people use the library. There is a free art gallery section open to anyone so you can peer around before deciding to join.

* Other private libraries offer an idiosyncratic mix of lovely old and new books and clubby services. Find your nearest or most useful private library from the Association of Independent Libraries, c/o The Leeds Library, 18 Commercial Street, Leeds, LS1 6AL. Send an ordinary SAE for a leaflet with a full list of members, or call 0113 245 3071.

MR THRIFTY'S WARDROBE

Clothes, like people, grow more interesting with age. A neat mend is an honourable thing. Wear it with pride. I sometimes patch clothes with contrasting fabric, usually upholstery samples given out free by Homebase, Habitat and Laura Ashley. To renew worn-out areas, you can buy iron-on leather patches and replacement pockets from haberdashers, who sometimes also sell underarm shields – shaped oval patches of neutral-coloured fabric. These throwbacks to the 1950s make clothes, especially silks, last much longer by preventing staining from perspiration and, more heinous, anti-perspirants.

Before discarding clothes into the ragbag for use as polishing cloths etc., remove and re-use buttons, ribbons and zips.

I buy many clothes from charity shops and car boot sales. You get the best quality clothes, especially for men, in Scotland, where the tweeds are thick and sturdy and they buy things to last.

You will buy the cream of the clothes from jumble sales by turning up early to help; you get a preview.

Fashionable clothes including sheepskin coats for less

Oxfam Originals is the name of Oxfam's fashion clothes-selling section for men and women. It has four shops in London and Manchester, and 35 shops-within-shops elsewhere, usually near universities. It's not dirt-cheap: expect to pay £35 for a sheepskin coat or duffel coat, or up to £50 for a leather jacket, while 1970s spangled and embroidered ball gowns and jeans come in cheaper and you can spy some couture labels too.

* 01865 313600 for your nearest branch.

Bargains at the factory door

I have re-lined my winter coat through my local cleaner at a cost of £20, and will be wearing it for another 10 years. If yours has worn out, take this tip from Barbara Nadel, a language lecturer who got it from her Greek and Turkish students. Every major town has its rag trade area – the clothes-making section. Wander round it and find the factories – not the wholesale shops, but the actual factories making things. Find the back door – always a good place for bargains in any industry – and ask what they are currently making. Get chatting and you may find yourself admitted to the magic circle of those offered luxury clothes like coats and baby clothes, kept as samples, at a tiny fraction of the shop price.

Make your own

I have recently refurbished my grandmother's Singer hand-operated sewing machine for £30 and have used it, at zero cost for electricity, to make clothes from paper patterns. In a local fabric shop, the prices of paper patterns averaged 50p and the material for party garb came in at all of £5.50, with the making time about half a day. I use pre-World War I thread, which is nice and strong, rescued from my grandmother's collection; this is the sort of treasure house-clearance firms will throw away, so contact them and ask. Die-hard thrifties can use all these points to extract conversation-value from their finished clothes at parties.

Lewisham & Deptford Sewing Machines has been selling sewing machines for over 50 years. 'Your best buy,' says Manager Tony Bulford, 'is an old hand Singer, which we sell for £20–£30. They go on and on, they're easy to repair, you can still get new parts, and they're beautiful ornaments too, some with mother of pearl inlays.' Treadle models, worked with your feet, start at £40. If you want to do a lot of sewing, curtains or upholstery, he suggests an old Singer electric industrial model, at around £100, which some customers buy to re-upholster their classic Jaguar E-type cars.

* 181 Deptford High Street, London, SE8 3NT, and branches. 020 8692 1077.

If you don't feel confident about making things for yourself, your local dry cleaner will charge you a lot less than a posh, professional dress-maker. Existing dresses can be cut down into skirts, or clothes widened or taken in or up, for £5–£10. If you buy anything at an expensive clothes shop, ask about alterations at the time. They can take things up, down, in and out for free – but only if you ask.

Wholesale bargains

The Market Trader or *The Trader* are magazines which list huge numbers of wholesalers or cash and carry stores around the country. Many of these wholesalers are not averse to selling to the walk-in general public. Order a copy from your newsagent.

Mending things without sewing

Textile Repair Powder is an iron-on glue which you use instead of sewing with thread. Sprinkle the powder, apply a hot iron, and the fabrics will fuse. £2.35 buys a 12g jar which covers 'a lot', says my spy. Other short cuts are iron-on Invisible Mending Tape, 99p a metre, and iron-on Wunderweb for hems at £1.89 for eight metres. To stop fabrics fraying, dab on Fraycheck, £3.25 for a small bottle, or try nail varnish.

* From haberdashers, including Maple Textiles, 189 Maple Road, London, SE20 8HT. 020 8778 8049.

TearMender is a latex-based liquid similar to that used by cleaners offering Invisible Mending. You paint it onto torn fabric and it dries quickly to a scarce-visible, waterproof bond. Also repairs soft-top cars and re-tips shoelaces, trumpet the makers.

* £9.99 plus p&p, *Innovations* mail order, 0870 908 7002 www.innovations.co.uk

Old clothes always dye rather than fade away

Dyeing clothes to restore them, make them more fashionable, or cover stubborn stains, is particularly popular with jeans wearers. Black jeans apparently go grey, but a small pack of Dylon machine dye, at around £4.50, will restore the colour. You can also perk up your furniture: those who have bought anything with a removable cover from Ikea, go crazy to dye it bright pink for some reason.

* Dylon consumer advice line, 020 8663 4296.

Cheap clothes

There are bargains for men and women, like coats for £9.99, at the Uncollected Dry Cleaning Shops, The Granger Market, Newcastle Upon Tyne (0191 232 6233) and The Metro Centre, Gateshead, Tyne & Wear (0191 460 3195).

More than cheap clothes

Cheap clothes and other interesting things can be bought at army surplus and camping shops. I love Lawrence Corner, where I have bought, among other things, a doctor's specimen jar to use as a vase, 50p and identical to those seen later in a Chelsea shop at a pricier price.

* 62 Hampstead Road, London NW1. 020 7813 1010.

Swopping clothes

If you have the nerve, take goodish clothes to stallholders at your local market and sell or swop them. You will also find local dress agencies in *Yellow Pages*, which will sell your clothes, taking a commission. Think ahead; people buy party clothes near Christmas, cooler clothes in spring and winter clothes in autumn.

Clothes recycled from the very rich

Sheila Warren-Hill sells dressy dresses and sometimes royal cast-offs from her North London home. She may offer you a glass of well-chilled champagne, lunch or tea in the garden, in a party atmosphere in which no one is pushed to buy. You can try her jacuzzi which rises in the air. Should you want to part with a lot of money, a masseuse stands by to ease the strain and, for £30 or so, give counselling for your life's woes too.

Sheila herself suggests shoes, coats and hats and jewellery to match outfits, even lending her own jewellery for special occasions. I know no better way to buy really top people's clothes for about a tenth of the price they paid for them. Many are not even worn if their first owners bought three in different colours and later decided they hated them all. Sheila also sends clothes to agencies nationwide.

* 020 8348 8282.

Home-made socks

Do you know your sock size? A properly fitting pair is more comfortable and lasts longer. Peta Flint creates individually hand-made socks, from £15.50 for a calf-length cable-knit ankle to £29.50 for full length shooting hose. Send an SAE for details.

* 246 Basford Road, Old Basford, Nottingham, NG6 0HY. Orders: 0115 978 2471.

Hand-made shoes

Made to measure shoes last 20 years and are particularly good if you have problem feet with bunions or fallen arches, as they will stop these worsening. Ask any old-fashioned cobbler, expect to pay £300 and wait six months.

James Taylor & Son customers are still wearing shoes made for them in the 1970s but the charge is £895 plus VAT, with subsequent pairs at least £100 less. They say all shoes last longer if you wear them on alternate days, as a rest gives a chance for perspiration to evaporate. Cleaning with proper wax is vital.

* 4 Paddington Street, London, W1M 3LA. 020 7935 5917.

Crispian Shoemakers are a charming family firm offering unique, 'natural'-shaped styles of shoes and boots which won't cramp toes. Popular with students because they will incorporate many colours in one shoe, the prices for made to measure start at £100.

* Wayside Cottage, Norton St Philip, Near Bath, BA3 6LT. 01373 834639.

* A list of made-to-measure shoemakers and shoes for special needs can be found in the booklet *Footwear For Special Needs*, £3 including p&p from the British Footwear Association, 5 Portland Place, London, W1N 3AA. 020 7580 8687.

Made-to-measure Savile Row suits at low prices

James & James (formerly tailors to the Duke of Windsor) make properly tailored suits at a third of the Savile Row price (from £585) by using a computer system into which your measurements are fed, so it laser-cuts the cloth, saving expense and time. Your suit is ready in two weeks, with one fitting needed.

* 11 Old Burlington Street, London, W1X 1LA. 020 7734 1748.

Hand-made Clothes at Hong Kong prices

Mr. Raja Daswanti of Raja fashions in Hong Kong regularly visits Britain to measure clients for hand-made suits, evening clothes, shirts, dresses, leather jackets and shoes, which are made in Hong Kong at a huge reduction, then sent within three weeks. Existing outfits can be copied or your own fabric made up. A man's suit costs from £139. You have to get on his mailing list and make an appointment.

* 34C Cameron Road, Kowloon, Hong Kong.
www.raja-fashions.com

Cheap bespoke tailoring for men and women without leaving home

A national, travelling tailor service is offered by 40 Savile Row, with savings of around £1500 on a made-to-measure traditional men's suit. If you can't go there to be measured, someone will visit you, digitally photograph you and log those details into the computer. They will also advise you on cut, colour, material, etc. and a vast array of details like cuffs. Suits are made to Savile Row hand-made standards in four weeks from £490. Shirts are from £69.

* 40 Savile Row, London W1X 1AG. 020 7287 6740
www.40savilerow.co.uk

Cheaper school uniform

Make friends with the mothers of older children at your child's school. You will be given cast-offs if you go about it the right way. Don't buy separate shorts for boys in summer – just cut down long trousers.

Stop vacuuming and start knitting

I am delighted with this tip from Celia Haddon. You can make clothing from the fur of pets and other animals, which you have gathered and saved. Look for a book called *Knitting with Dog Hair (Better a sweater from a dog you know and love than a sheep you'll never meet)* by Kendall Crolius (Hutchinson, £6.99) with instructions for mittens, sweaters and even a pillbox hat from your cat.

Mrs Pam Gardner spins dog, angora rabbit or cat fur into knittable wool. She charges from £9 per

100g of finished wool from dogs and from £11 for cats and stresses that you must only send long hairs, i.e. from one to two inches, and no tangles, dirt or fleas, please. They must be combings, not cuttings. A sweater works out at about £60, but of course a cushion is much cheaper.

* 1 Norton Crescent, Towcester, NN12 6DW. 01327 350025.

Fireproofing anything cheaply
Flamecheck is the stuff used by film people to fireproof a set. They say it will even make a paper handkerchief proof against a flame. You can spray it on anything. £12 per litre to cover 100 square feet.

* For stockists, call 01234 766788.

Ready-made clothes
TK Maxx are an astonishingly cheap source of designer-type clothes and presents, with 60 per cent off clothes. 01707 260066 for branches. Matalan is another such. 01708 864350 for branches.

Buying ex-hire shirts and suits
Hire shops sell off their smart suits and shirts while they are still reasonably presentable and I

have heard of shirts sold for 50p. Shephard &
Woodward, of Oxford, charge £5 for a dress
shirt in their January sale, for instance. Ask at
other hire shops.

* 109 High Street, Oxford, OX1 4BT. 01865 249491.

At least 60 per cent off couture clothes, shoes and fabrics

Designer Warehouse Sales is a London-based
organisation offering discounts on designer
clothes, shoes, underwear and fabrics at 14
annual sales, six each for men and women and
two for fabrics. There is a £2 entrance charge;
inside, each sale has 80 stands.

These sales are used by designers like Donna
Karan, Nicole Farhi, Ghost, and lingerie
makers like La Perla, to sell off the current
season's surplus stocks, cancelled orders and,
best value of all, one-off, beautifully-tailored
catwalk samples worn once by the model.
Reductions are at least 60 per cent. Women
will find the best bargains in sizes 10 to 12,
and shoe size seven, because this is the model's
standard size.

The fabric sales are gems for those who can make
things, or get them made, if you like very high-
class, hand-painted velvets by, say, Georgina Von
Etzdorf, or sheepskins. One customer bought

enough sheepskin for a bedspread, £35 the lot.
Remnants start at 50p.

* Free mailing list for advance information, 020 7704 1064 or
www.dwslondon.co.uk

Cheap dry cleaning
Home dry cleaning kits, which you use in a
tumble dryer, merely claim to 'freshen' clothes,
which you can do for free by hanging them on
a line in the fresh air. You'll get better value
from launderette dry cleaning machines. You
can save pounds off your professional dry
cleaning bills by realising that prices vary
immensely by area, even if the cleaner is part
of a national, well-known chain. I always use
dry cleaners in cheap parts of town.

VANITY, THY NAME IS MR THRIFTY

South America is the world test-market for toiletries because they consume more toiletries per head than anyone else in the world. If you want to test some new products at low prices, take a holiday there.

Don't pour money down the drain

Bath salts soften and scent the water, but the herbs or magic ingredient they contain are in amounts too tiny to do anything medicinal to you. Salt, dissolved in the water, is cheaper and a natural antiseptic. Baby oil, scented if you like with a few drops of your perfume, is a cheap natural moisturising bath oil; it does as more expensive oils do, which is to sit on the water and cling to your skin when you rise, like Venus from the waves.

Save money on expensive skin cream

The cheapest effective skincare I have found is Boots Cucumber, £1.19 each for a cleanser or moisturiser. Don't assume that an expensive cream costs a lot because it works. Its makers will ask the price they think they can get away with. I know this, because I used to write skin cream adverts when I was young and giddy. Makers would test new potions by asking women how much they were prepared to pay, then doubling it.

Save money by not buying 'skin toners'. I have never got to the bottom of what they do, or why you should want something to close your pores before you put on a moisturiser which you want to sink into your skin.

Home-made beauty from your kitchen cupboard

From *The Beauty Manual* by Sandra Morris (Weidenfeld and Nicolson, £14.99) comes the interesting idea that food colouring, of the kind you buy in tubes for icing, will stain your lips for longer than lipstick at a fraction of the price. She also suggests beetroot lip stain, but, much as I adore eating it, I can't imagine anyone wanting to be close to you after a time because of the smell. Apparently, toothpaste and lemon juice both zap spots and almond oil nourishes nails.

Money off make-up and toiletries

Direct Cosmetics sells drastically discounted make-up, skincare, suncare, perfumes, nail varnish, gift sets, even brushes and jewellery by post. 'This stuff is pukka and new,' says owner Bill Doody, who has been trading for 21 years and

is a leading member of the Parallel Traders'
Association, a group of sellers who buy in bulk
abroad where things are cheaper.

It's not like going into a posh perfume
department. You receive a massive postal list and
you can't guarantee to find the very thing you
want that month. Brands available vary from
Ralph Lauren to Superdrug. Examples of price
cuts include Lancôme foundation, £16 in the
shops, £2.45 to you. Versace Blonde perfume at
£24.50, normally £56. Even day-to-day bathroom
things like Clearasil come in at £2.45, against £3.99
in the high street. Sally Hansen nail varnish
normally costs £3.95 per bottle; Direct Cosmetics
sells a bag of ten for that price.

* Long Row, Oakham, Rutland, LE15 6LN. 01572 756805. Or order
through their website, www.directcosmetics.com

Free samples

Perfume counters of any big store are always good
for a free top-up of the latest scent if you feel life
has lost its fragrance. Liberty's is my favourite for
free samples from esoteric, unusual perfume
houses. The staff are happy to give away little
bottles if they have them; otherwise, they spray
sample sniffs on cards which you can use to scent
your handkerchief drawers.

* 210–220 Regent Street, London, W1F 6AH. 020 7734 1234.

You will also find luxury lotions and perfumes in the lavatories of luxury hotels, and department stores like Harvey Nichols, Knightsbridge, London SW1.

Cheap perfume

The Perfume Shop sells all perfumes at a discount, even the normally impossible-to-find-cheaply Chanel or Estée Lauder, both companies that fiercely protect their prices. The Perfume Shop quoted £41.75 for Chanel No 5 Eau de Parfum against Selfridge's £48.

If your favourite fragrance has been discontinued, it will try to find any remaining stocks for you. If this fails, or you fancy a change, the staff can help you choose another one using a chart of similar and related fragrances. If you are choosing a gift, the staff will make a recommendation based on questions like the recipient's age, occupation, hair colour and personality.

* 01494 539900 for branches and phone advice.

Cheap beauty treatments

Women and men can get every beauty treatment – the latest and most luxurious included – free or extremely cheaply by allowing supervised students to practise on them. The only charge is for materials. I always leave a tip.

What's available depends on the time of year. September is least good because new students are still learning skills, but by Christmas there are plenty of opportunities to treat yourself to whole days of beauty therapy.

* Contact your nearest College of Technology or anywhere that offers a beauty therapy course.

The London College of Fashion offers all beauty therapies most days, and they are a few pounds cheaper if a first-year student does them. A basic facial is £3, waxing from £2.50, aromatherapy massage £10, electro-epilation (hair removal) £1, manicure £2.50, and non-surgical micro-current face-lift facial £10. Cathiodermie massage is £7.

* 20 John Princes Street, London, W1M 0BJ. Ring 020 7514 7400 and ask for Beauty Reception.

The Steiner School of Beauty Therapy offers low-price treats on Tuesdays, Wednesdays and Thursdays. Send SAE for the price list. A special occasion make-up or facial with make-up is perfect for parties, £9.40. Desincrustation facial with galvanic currents to remove impurities, £7 to you. Vibro-massage slimming is £6.30, a manicure £4.90, and top-to-toe massage, facial, manicure and pedicure comes in at £23. (This only at 2pm on Tuesdays, and 10am and 2pm on Wednesdays and Thursdays.)

* 193 Wardour Street, London, W1V 3FA. 020 7434 4534.

Cheap therapeutic massage

For a proper therapeutic massage, the London College of Massage offers treatment for aches and pains from senior students costing £15 for a two-hour session (normal cost £45). You may have to ask to go on the waiting-list but it won't be long. You get a half-hour chat about your aches and pains, then they decide to give you a Swedish-based technique, a neck massage or whatever.

* 5 Newman Passage, London, W1P 3PF. 020 7637 7125.

For an hour's shiatsu massage from senior students, try the London College of Shiatsu. It costs £10. You must book in advance at well-supervised clinics for senior students to try out their skills; held every three weeks.

* 25–27 Dalling Road, London, W6 0JD. 020 8741 3323.

How to get a top hair-do for free

Top hairdressers are constantly looking for 'models', male and female, to have their hair done free. If you have a particular salon which you're desperate to try, but which normally charges over £100 a head, give them a ring and ask. You needn't be 19 and stick-thin, merely not mind having your hair pulled around by trainees – or if you're willing to travel further and turn up for competitions, examinations or demonstrations, you might get an Artistic Director. You can get everything from a trim to a perm or colour in the latest fashion, though it will take longer than an ordinary appointment and may be in the evening. You can also try your local salon.

* Saks is a 70-salon group from Brighton to Edinburgh which seeks 'models' of all ages and both sexes. For your nearest branch phone 01325 380333; but if you pop your head round the door of any salon, they won't say no, though they might ask you to come back later.

* Toni & Guy Academy in London offers both-sex hair-dos at two different training-schools with appointments at 9.45 or 1.45 daily. 'Classic' (020 7486 4733) should be your destination if you want a trim, bob or accepted cut like a 'square layer', or one colour or highlights. 'Advanced' (020 7836 0606) is your place for avant garde colours and experimental haircuts. Either way, it costs £5 but is free with a coupon from the free magazines *Miss London* or *GAT*, which you find given out at big London rail and tube stations on Monday mornings.

* Mersey-based hairdressing school Andrew Collinge runs refresher hairdressing courses for those already in the business and needs models for free haircuts (no perms or colouring). Expect to be there from 1.30 to 4.30. 0151 709 5942. You get a quicker, reduced-price haircut from the Training Salon, 0151 709 4848.

* Regis has a group of over 350 nationwide salons, including Hair Express, Master Cuts and Trade Secrets, some of which also offer beauty treatments. 024 7684 0300.

Cutting your own hair

With common sense and a small, sharp pair of scissors, you can cut hair yourself. Here are some tips from a hairdressing manual:

- Comb the hair first and cut it the way it falls naturally.
- If cutting wet, remember, hair dries shorter.
- Centre partings and short hair make round faces, double chins and big noses look bigger.
- Keep control by cutting in small sections, starting at the crown and working out.
- For a layered look, hold hair straight out from head and cut 180° down.
- To cut a fringe, hold your finger straight across your forehead as a guide.

With the cheapest haircut around £5 in a shop, if you have much hair or many heads to shear, invest in an electric home haircutting device. The cheapest I have found is by Visiq, £8.99 from Argos (0870 600 1010 for your nearest store/mail order). I tested Wahl's 300 haircutter (£19.99 from Argos), which comes in a smart case with an armoury of attachments and a video. I ignored that and just ran the trimmer over my guinea pig. Human, not animal. It was fine.

Savings on bathroom basics

Supersave Drugstore is the cheapie shop group

set up by Lloydspharmacy. It offers to undercut supermarket and other chemists on 200 basic toiletries.

M.D. Graham Bispham explained that they employ someone full-time to tour Boots, Superdrug and the supermarkets checking 200 'opinion-forming prices' – the things you and I pretty much know the price of. They also try to undercut small stores operating on the grey market, selling imported things like overseas versions of well-known brands, very cheap. 'Duty-free perfume prices are not as good as people imagine,' he adds. 'We take £6 to £10 off around 17 men's and women's fragrances each month, especially at Christmas.'

* 01203 432 090 for your nearest store.

Longer-lasting deodorant
A reader of *Tightwad Gazette*, an American publication, recycles ends of solid deodorant stick to make a new one – four ends will make a new stick, apparently. She dug out the bits with a knife, put them in a cup and microwaved on a very cool setting until they melted together, then put the resultant goo into a container and left it to cool.

This is a modern spin on the old-fashioned technique of gently heating old soap ends in a saucepan to make a new bar, and it can be adapted for old lipsticks, especially when a favourite colour has been discontinued.

Or try Deodorant Stone. Mine has lasted me five years. This mystical-looking, ice-blue, potassium sulphate rock works by inhibiting the growth of smelly bacteria, coating skin invisibly. It does not clog up your pores like cheap deodorant, nor stop you perspiring. Nor does it contain aluminium chlorohydrate, which is generally considered undesirable. You can also use it for your feet.

* £5 (plus £2.50 p&p if mail ordered), Neal's Yard Remedies, 0161 831 7875 for mail order; 020 7627 1949 for stockists.

Free expert advice and top quality cosmetics for less than high street prices

Glauca Rossi, the top make-up artist, is struck by how much money women waste on lipsticks and eye make-up which they buy as a shot in the dark, without knowing what they will look like on their face.

Send her a close-up snapshot of yourself and she will advise on what colours you should wear on your face, free. Then, should you wish, you can buy make-up from her private range of around 100 items, displayed in a catalogue at knock-down, mail-order prices. These were developed for professional makeup artists and are not available in the shops. A lipstick costs £5.25; a double eye shadow palette £7 – and, she says, they stay on for a long time.

The cosmetics are personally developed by Glauca and a chemical specialist and made by a top manufacturer. The technical specifications match many big names, with non-irritant ingredients, not tested on animals.

This own label is so cheap because she does not use expensive packaging, nor does she advertise, though the palettes are generous and strong enough for everyday use by professionals and have mirrors and sponge applicators included.

* The Glauca Rossi School of Make-up, 10 Sutherland Avenue, London W9. 020 7289 7485.

Getting free samples from shops

Go to any cosmetics counter in a big store and say something like, 'I'm not sure about my skin/foundation/lipstick' (even if you're a man), and you will be showered with advice, offers of free makeovers or skin sessions, and free samples. Try Lancôme and Estée Lauder especially.

Body Shop offers makeovers for £10, hand or footcare, or can concentrate on just eyes or lips in half an hour, or 10 minutes if you say you're in a hurry. Avoid busy times, Saturdays and lunchtimes. You may have to make an appointment.

Penhaligon's mail order always adds an extra free phial of scent with an order. Better still, £5 buys a 'scent library' of 13 phials, for men or for women, of every fragrance they offer, including the 'gender free' Quercus.

* Units 5–7, Blenheim Court, Brewery Road, London, N7 9NY. 0800 716108.

Becoming a tester

Lush is the reincarnation of an off-beat hair, face and bath goodies company formerly called Cosmetics to Go. It has shops and a mail-order operation. I bought some hair preparation which made my hair look like a birds' nest – so I wrote asking for a refund. I received this plus an invitation to join their testing panel, together with a massive box of goodies. This was a curate's egg (good in parts), as the first thing I tested was some bath stuff containing bits of leaf which blocked my drains expensively. However on the whole, the plusses outweighed the minuses.

Other cosmetics companies may prove equally responsive, especially if you have some particular quality to offer them for testing, like a sensitive skin.

* Lush Retail, 01202 667830

MR THRIFTY EATS OUT

Look out for the *Financial Times* and other newspapers' annual foodfests – collect the tokens and get Lunch for a Fiver at many top restaurants.

However, my favourite night out ever was at a restaurant which was by day someone's front room in a tiny terraced house. Our chef showed us the contents of his fridge and we chose what we wanted, based on what he had. Whilst waiting, I admired polaroid snaps of various tatty Land Rovers labelled 'Our Travel Service to Morocco'. The restaurant-in-a-house was no doubt closed down by killjoy health authorities.

***Belgo Restaurants' Bierdrome Brasseries offer a two-course, steak-frites – style lunch at £5.00. A loyalty card gives you the fifth lunch free.
020 7209 2176 for details.**

Eating out

The cheapest good meals I've had recently have been from hospital canteens. Not the smarty-pants cafés selling croissants at cardiac arrest prices, but the scruffier staff canteens, open till late to cater for overworked medical staff. Desperate to make ends meet, most are happy to see ordinary visitors. Though you don't get the staff discount, you will find old-fashioned canteen style steak and chips or vegetarian meals and good ethnic dishes for bargain prices.

If you visit often, I suggest repaying the hospital by taking up voluntary hospital visiting or serving in trolley shops for the odd hour, through the hospital's Friends organisation.

The other cheap eating places are youth hostels. Those in central-city locations like Bristol stay open all day, offering all-comers well-cooked café meals for measly prices.

* YHA information line, 0870 870 8808.

How to find out about diners' discounts

Restaurant Services is a free advice and information service covering every restaurant in London. They advise on the best places and best deals for you, from business lunches and romantic dinners à deux to stag or hen parties and wedding buffets. They say they are always ahead with news of special events like food festivals or promotions like Valentine's Day.

If you want what they call a 'faster, prestige' service, £35 a year buys you private membership, and £70 corporate membership for up to four people. You receive a monthly newsletter with restaurant gossip, special offers and discounts, and invitations to private opening parties.

* Monday to Friday, 9am to 7pm. 020 8888 8080.

How to give a bit of a do for a bit less of a bill
Catering colleges usually have restaurants at which catering students try out their cooking and waiting skills. The costs are less than a conventional restaurant and the service is attentive, though the decor is often a bit drab and old-fashioned.

One such is Hospitality/Catering at Chichester College of Art, Science and Technology, which quotes £25 per head for a three-course meal including all wines, and says it feasts a lot of feasting organisations and local businesses.

* 01243 786321.

Bottomless tea and coffee pots

Little Chef offers free fill-ups for all-in prices. So does Porters, the Earl of Bradford's English restaurant (17 Henrietta Street, London WC1). My preference is to sink into the cushions of top hotels for coffee – never as expensive as it looks, and they also have clean lavatories. The Savoy, Strand, London WC2 charges £3.80 for a cafétière of coffee, containing three cups, which makes it competitive with Pizza Hut.

MR THRIFTY DRIVES A HARD BARGAIN

Walking and cycling are cheap, healthy, ecologically friendly but increasingly dangerous. Public transport is expensive, inconvenient and risky. The RAC estimates that a family saves £1000 a year per year not using public transport. I wish someone would set up a company of cheap, go-anywhere, people carrier taxis, which circle a set area making up the route as they go along according to who gets on, and drop you at your front door.

Meanwhile, I shall hire a pair of roller blades at £4 for the first hour and £1 per hour after that.

* 020 7928 6838. www.londonbicycle.com

Minicab lore

If you take minicabs, agree a price beforehand on the phone. Minicab drivers pay a weekly fee to their companies and then charge what they can get away with. If you have a regular trip, negotiate a fixed price first with 'the office'. It is wise to pretend to be saying goodbye to someone at your door in sight of a minicab driver. I once had a driver who pointed out the 'sights' en route – the places he had burgled.

Save time and money by employing a 'driving au pair'

If you have many errands, trips, school runs and children to take to numerous social engagements, rather than acting as unpaid driver, a time-and cost-saving may be to employ an au pair or similar young person, say from Australia or South Africa, mainly for driving the family. Instead of traditional au pair babysitting duties, they might take and collect you from evening appointments on occasions, so that you can drink at parties.

At bed, board and around £45 a week for pocket money, you may save on taxis and parking. Check your car insurance position; some insurers consider that a driver who is not part of your family is 'professional' and your insurance bills go up.

Young people travelling from Australia tend to have driving licences and a responsible attitude and are allowed to work for a year. You should pay for them to have a refresher driving course over here. A friend, Juliet Moxley, who has employed au pairs for years, suggests offering them a significant sum like £200 at the end of their stay on condition they have not had an accident. 'It works and it's cheaper than losing your no claims bonus,' she explains.

The costs of hiring an au pair, even if they look after you or your children or even your elderly parent, are lower than traditional care assistants or nannies, nor do you have to pay national insurance or other taxes. According to a table issued by the International Au Pair Association, male au pairs are cheaper than female ones – their weekly pocket money seems to average £30 to women's £45. For an 'au pair plus' who works longer hours, you could save £30 on the women's fee of £70. I don't know why this should be, although if you have a live-in mother's help, the cost is the same – from £100.

* Expect to pay an au pair agency at least £50 for its finding service, and up to £395 for a long-term au pair. The cheapest au pair agency I have found is IAPO, a free service which asks for a £20 donation: 22 The Ridings, Norwich, NR4 6UJ. E-mail iapo@au-pair.org

* Others to try include Global Au Pairs, 020 8467 6092, e-mail request@au-pairs.co.uk. Childcare International Ltd, 020 8906 3116, e-mail office@childint.co.uk; Au Pair and Student Placement Agency, 01785 780424, e-mail aspa@uk-hq.demon.co.uk

* Au pair agencies should be members of regulatory bodies. The Universal Au Pair Association is based at PO Box 1332, Gallo Manor, 2052 South Africa, fax 27-11-804-6248, infoeuapa.org. The International Au Pair Association is at Bredgade 25H, 1260 Copenhagen, Denmark, telephone 45 333 39600. The International Fellowship of Au Pair Agencies is on 01785 780424.

Choose a safe car

According to a table compiled by *What Car?* magazine in 1999, the best thief-proof cars are the £22,000 Lexus IS200, followed by BMW 323Ci, 328i and 520i, then Ford Focus 1.6 estate and 5-door models. Bottom of the list came Audi's A3 1.8T and A4 2.8.

Don't buy a new car at the quoted price

A dealer's minimum profit is 10 per cent. Make an offer or ask for a discount. S/he will expect this question. Play him off against another dealer. 'So-and-so offered *this* much off.' Salesmen, like lovers, adore the excitement of a chase.

Buying a car from abroad

From Alfa Romeo to Citroën Xantia, British-specification right-hand drive cars are available from foreign dealers at massive savings, sometimes up to £10,000.

Broadspeed helps ordinary people to help themselves to such savings. Its answerphone message is a model of clarity and helpfulness, and explains everything you need to know about how to buy a car abroad.

Broadspeed offers services costing from £10 to £1000 to help you through the entire car-buying process, depending on how confident you feel about buying a car abroad with their advice.

£10 buys its *DIY Car Importers' Guide*, your car-buyer's Bible. This lists Broadspeed-friendly dealers abroad, and helps you to find the make and dealer you want and the right country to buy from by balancing cut-prices against waiting time for your car.

Once you have decided, Broadspeed adds that its dealers can often offer extra discounts too, so do your homework. You must also make sure that you get the pan-European service warranty so that your car can be serviced in Britain. Some makers won't allow this, making their cars impossible to import cheaply. Impossible to import at a saving are Ferrari, Lexus, Mitsubishi, Seat and Isuku.

Broadspeed can help you book a ferry to do the whole thing yourself at less than £20 each way through the various Car Cruise Partners (P&O, Stena, DFDS). Or it can help you with specific parts of the process, like collecting the car for you, at perhaps £700. It can do the whole thing at a top cost of £1000 – all prices plus VAT.

The online service at www.car-prices.com will allow you to buy the guide and lead you to finance and ways of selling your existing car online if necessary.

* Recorded information on 020 8387 9121. Buy the guide, known as

Option One, for £10 (cheques payable to Broadspeed) from Steps Farm, Rectory Hill, Polstead, Colchester, CO6 5AE. Fax your request to 01206 263454, together with your credit card details, including expiry date and issue number. Advice and help from a proper living person are on hand Monday to Friday, 9–6, at £1 per minute, so have your query well-honed. 0906 960888; 0906 9608880.

Buying an imported car without travelling abroad

You can buy a cheaper imported car by proxy through one of the Parallel trading car companies in Britain. You get the advantage that you can trade-in your old car and also use finance deals easily and by talking to a person in this country.

Park Lane (UK) Ltd is one example. Bargains they mentioned to me included a Hyundai Atos people carrier in any colour and with higher specification features like central locking and electric windows, for £5995 on the road, saving around £1300 on the list price. Another deal was a new Porsche 996 for £59,995, saving £10,000, and Mercedes Smart cars at a saving of £1000. These are all new right-hand drive cars with warranties of up to three years, depending on the car.

'We don't just buy from importers, and we're not tied to franchisers. We're global car dealers, buying in bulk and taking advantage of currency fluctuations,' explained their Sean Lockyer. 'We buy where there are opportunities: for instance, taxation laws change so that a small-engined car isn't so saleable, or where a consignment of cars has been left on the dock for some reason.'

You can't 'order' a car to your exact specifications this way. You must be flexible, not too fussy about details like colour, as if you are buying a secondhand car. Sean suggests looking up the current stock on the website if you can before phoning.

* Park Lane (UK) Ltd, Omega Park, Alton, Hants, GU34 2YU. 01420 544300, www.park-lane.co.uk

* For other members of the Parallel trading motor trade, call BIMTE, 01925 244120. For up to £1000 off all makes of motorcycle, try 01159 301321 (Granby Motors); if you have any difficulty finding the machine you want, call wholesaler Jack Glover on 01159 326986 for help.

Save thousands on a new or secondhand car

Go to a car broker. Like an insurance broker, s/he charges nothing to shop around on your behalf, using buying power for company fleets to get ordinary customers cut-price deals.

Brokers advertise in car magazines. Phone a few. You're not limited to those in your vicinity, since you won't visit them. You can ask for a quote on a specific make, with its colour and mileage, or a recommendation within your price range. Test drive a few cars at a showroom before you decide.

Don't give a deposit or pay for the car before you see it. The broker may claim to belong to the MAA (the dealers' organisation) but it's no guarantee. Check that your car is not a left-hand drive and that it's driveable straight away; you don't want to pay to do things like adjust the headlamps.

You should be able to collect your new car from a main showroom, as if you bought it from them, but before getting to that stage, have a written confirmation of the price. Check that the broker has legal title to the car. Unscrupulous types may turn up and demand cash on your doorstep, then vamoose, leaving you pursued by an irate dealer who hasn't been paid.

Cover yourself by asking the broker for the name of the dealer from whom you will collect the car, checking with that dealer that they have a business relationship with the broker, and paying the dealer direct. Bona fide brokers won't mind this.

One longstanding broker, Vehicle Sourcing Ltd, says: 'We give impartial advice. We have no axe to grind, especially to ladies who aren't sure what car to have. We suggest makes they may not have considered. And we have a vested interest in selling good cars, because we like to see our customers come back and part-exchange later.'

* **01865 358921.**

A company who will buy a secondhand car at auction for you

Auctions can save considerable sums. Julian Trim & Co. are specialists in buying cars at auction and take a six per cent mark-up, not the 20 per cent dealers take for secondhand cars. You tell them exactly what you seek and they supply a written quote and order form. You return it with £100 deposit. They find the car, phone you with a description on auction day, and suggest a likely price and bidding limits. If you don't like it, you don't pay, but they keep the £100 for their time.

* 01747 838888.

Buying a car over the Internet

Not as easy as it seems. The process should start with checking websites like *Top Gear* and *What Car* for reviews of what's new. Then go to the car manufacturer's site to check the prices, specifications and special offers. Finally, look at a few dealers' sites to see what discounts and delivery times are available. If you buy over the net, the dealer will visit you with your chosen car, value your existing car for part-exchange and give you a test drive. You need not commit yourself then and there; you can go back to the screen and order the car later, or start again.

When I tested all this, I found the Top Gear site mysteriously led me to seller Autobytel, which rushed me through a process. I nearly agreed to buy a £50,000 Mercedes I didn't want, with no way of going back.

Car makers will all have websites: check deals like Vauxhall's, offering £1000 saving on a new car through the Internet. As far as dealers go, Oneswoop claims to offer 40 per cent off new cars from Ford, Peugeot, Rover and VW by sourcing them through Europe. Totalise offers savings of over £3000 on new Fords plus three years' roadside recovery from Green Flag. American company Autobytel sells most makes of new and used car over the Internet.

Oneswoop has teamed with Marks & Spencer Financial Services to offer you finance for cars bought from Europe. The service is initially limited to Audi, Ford, General Motors, Peugeot, Rover and BMW and connects you to dealers throughout Europe, with the car being delivered to your door.

* www.vauxhall.co.uk; www.totalise.net; www.autobytel.co.uk; www.oneswoop.com; www.gmbuypower.com (General Motors only); carpoint.nsn.com (n.b. *no* www. before address); members.aol.com/cars 305/carsdir

Drive a secondhand cab
A secondhand black cab as your personal car is cheap and beneficial if you drive a lot in town, as cab owner Prince Philip does. You're not

supposed to use the fast bus and taxi lanes to bypass jams, but who's to know? You get a solid, well-maintained vehicle, good in a crash, with excellent brakes and turning circle, doing around 25 miles to the gallon of diesel.

Cabs are mostly sold at around eight years old, and one with around 28,000 miles on the clock should cost something like £3000. A 15-year-old vehicle with a year's MOT, but no warranty, costs £750 from North Eastern Motors, East London, but perhaps it's more prudent to pay upwards of £1000 for a cab with a six-month warranty covering parts and labour.

* North Eastern Motors, Arch 79, Dunbridge Street, London E2. 020 7739 4043. Or the garages on Three Colt Street, London E1.

Check your car before you buy

Having a secondhand car's registration document does not mean the seller is the legal owner. If the car was leased, the leasing company will trace you and you'll have to make up the payments to them or lose it. It is easy, when buying, to check the car's chassis number – there are two sites, one roughly under the bonnet on the driver's side wing and the other at the feet of the driver near where the carpet begins, and both numbers should match.

HPI Autodata holds a national register of cars stolen, or with outstanding finance agreements, or which have been in major crashes. Call with your proposed car's registration number and chassis number and for £31 they will check it in minutes. About a third of all cars they are asked about have a problem.

* **01722 422422**

 Call 01722 422422 quoting Mr Thrifty and HPI Autodata will offer £5.00 off their HPI check, until the end of 2001.

Get the car inspected before buying
The AA (0800 783 4610) charges non-members from £175 for a full inspection before you buy a car, of which the first part is a 'history' check (as HPI's). If the car is a bad one, you only pay £31 and the test doesn't proceed. The RAC also has inspection services but with more complicated categories. 0870 533 3660 for details.

Cheap motorcycles
Motorcycles are cheaper to tax and insure and you get free parking in most city centres.

For rock-bottom prices, think East European. Ignore the advice of flashier riders and go for 125 or 250cc MZ (was German, now Turkish), 350cc Jawa (Czech) or 650cc Cossack/Dnieper/Ural (Russian). All three are well supported with dealers and spares. They are also long-lived in the right hands: unlike cars there is no inevitable decay through rust. If you buy these bikes secondhand, prices are on the floor. However, you are taking a chance on the previous owner's skill as a mechanic. The solution is to plan ahead and invest £12 or so to join one of the owner's clubs. All publish bi-monthly newsletters with bikes for sale in the back; prices will be good and there is a better chance that the seller's dipstick will be touching the oil.

* MZ Riders Club Membership Secretary: John Juckes/Anne-Marie Whitwell, 26 Eastfield Close, Tadcaster, North Yorkshire, LS24 8JX. E-mail: john@juckes.demon.co.uk

* Cossack Owners Club Membership Secretary: Alan Mottram, 19 The Villas, Stoke-on-Trent, ST4 5AQ. 01782 845035.

If you need to transport aged relatives, children, dogs, heavy shopping or tradesmen's tools, the cheapest form of powered transport is a motorcycle and sidecar. Do not buy both parts separately and marry them together; it's cheaper and easier to get one already assembled. The MZs, Jawas and Cossacks already mentioned are also famous as sidecar pullers; look in the club magazines for well-sorted examples.

Getting rescued
Never let the Police get your car towed off the

motorway. The charge is a minimum of £105 plus mileage. If you break down on a motorway, if safe, use the emergency phones, not your mobile. The Police can instantly tell where you are and send a patrol car to guard you if you are in any danger. Always carry a torch and a blanket.

If you are without a rescue service, a garage costs at least £40 to come to your aid and you're its helpless victim when it comes to repair charges. Rescue services like the AA and RAC now offer different levels of cover – from basic roadside rescue to overnight hotel accommodation if stranded, to help on holiday in Europe. You can cut the cost by paying through direct debit, racking up no claims bonuses (with the RAC for instance) or negotiating cheaper cover for a second car. Over-50s should check Saga for discounts; car club members, check the RAC.

Never be parted from your car if it needs returning home for a garage's attention; I once let the AA drive my car to one of its depots, where it languished for over a week before being returned.

Look at smaller rescue services. Britannia Rescue came out very well in a Consumers Association survey and does not limit the number of call-outs, even for old cars. Also look at Europ Assistance's UK Driver Assist (01444 442211), Green Flag (0806 00011), and the Environmental

Transport Association (01932 828882). Gem
Recovery advertises a no-frills service at £48.

* Gem (The Guild of Experienced Motorists), Station Road, Forest
Row, East Sussex, RH18 5EN. 0645 645 505.
www.gemrecovery.co.uk

The RAC has launched a new breakdown service
called Red. You pay £1 a month and are only
charged when you break down – a fixed fee of £49,
including 'home start'. However, when I spoke to
an RAC salesman, he pointed out that it was
cheaper to wait till you break down, then join at
the roadside for £43.

* www.redrac.com 0870 733 7222.

Car insurance
No one insurance company is best for everyone. Each
has preferred types of people, areas and cars, though
direct insurers you contact yourself, like Direct Line
(020 8253 8818) are considered competitive.

Direct Line offers monthly instalments at no extra
cost for home and car insurance. There are knock-
on benefits. If you take out their comprehensive car
insurance, you save 50 per cent on their rescue
service, which is run by the admirable Europ
Assistance. That would mean paying £38 for the
service, which they compare to the AA's £126 and
the RAC's £136.

Don't look for the cheapest policy. Check the excess (the money you pay yourself before the insurer gives a refund) and the claims service. Some insurers also offer a free Green Card, free breakdown services and free uninsured loss recovery. Norwich Union offers a free in-car, automatic map-reading device too.

Car insurance: how to watch it come down

Take extra tests. Pass Plus is a Government-backed extra driving scheme, available through motoring schools, which demands that you do six extra hours of observed driving in difficult conditions like rain and darkness. BSM quoted me a price of £119.94 for it. Having Pass Plus enables new drivers to secure reductions of between 25 and 40 per cent on an insurance premium.

Experienced drivers can take the Institute of Motorists' Advanced Driving Test. If you drive under 12,000 miles a year, some insurers (like AON Risk Services – 0800 001310) will lower your premium. The test alone costs £45; instruction with an approved motoring school near you, £75 including test.

* 020 8994 4403 for details.

Don't use your car to travel to work each day. Keeping it in a garage or drive is worth 10 per cent off too.

Don't drive a smart car. The insurance will be massive, it is more likely to be stolen or clamped, and other drivers are jealous; no one will let you into a queue of traffic.

Immobilisers, car tracking devices, deadlocks and alarms can get you up to 20 per cent off but check with the insurer first; they stipulate different devices.

Quotes are lower for women than men. If you are a couple, insure in the woman's name, with the man as an add-on driver. Many insurers give women a discount of up to 20 per cent. You may get special terms from Diamond (0800 362436) or Norwich Union Direct's Lady Motoring (0800 888111).

If you have two cars, don't lump them into the same policy. If one car is used for commuting, tell the insurer that the other car is only driven for social, domestic or pleasure uses, qualifying for a discount of from 5 to 10 per cent. If your second car is a sporty weekend car, like a Porsche or a classic car, a specialist or owners' club policy may be cheaper, especially if you agree to limited mileage, say under 3000 miles, and if you don't put a teenage driver's name on the policy. If you have a third car, insurers will assume it is for a young person and weight the premium accordingly.

If you are in a family, and you all drive the car, insure in the older person's name. If you are young and live a rather uncertain lifestyle, changing flats and in inner city areas, insure the car from your family home. But you must tell the truth or your policy is void.

Don't use 'any driver' policies. Limit the number of drivers using the car.

Insurance brokers are often no more expensive than the prices you get by going to an insurer direct and they also know insurance companies you don't, like Iron Trades, which specialises in third party, fire and theft policies, or Highway, which offers special terms to drivers with convictions.

The insurer may just charge you the same price and make extra profit from pocketing the commission. Brokers can get you the best bargains and save you the tedium of shopping around. In the event of a dispute with your insurers, you're on your own if you insure direct. An intermediary has more muscle and will fight for you.

* The AA is the biggest telephone broker. 0800 444 777. Autodirect 0800 731 1805; www.autodirect.co.uk guarantees lowest rates.

Online insurance

Insurers ironsure.com says it will find you the
right deal based on price, service and convenience,
with a helpline and 24-hour telephone reporting
service. The policy is paid for monthly, so you can
insure your car month-by-month rather than
annually, but you don't get refunds for cancelling
halfway through the month.

* Also try www.carquote.co.uk

Cut-price petrol

Sainsbury's used to claim its petrol as at least 15p
a litre cheaper than surrounding competitors, but
now Esso has launched its Pricewatch it's not so
sure. I can safely say that supermarket petrol
stations will offer reliably good value.

Servicing

Be clear when briefing mechanics. I foolishly told
one to 'do everything', only to be charged for
making the glove compartment fit more snugly. If
you are a woman, it might pay to get a man to talk
to them, any man, even if he is incompetent and
you are nudging him and asking all the serious
questions.

Get a pre-MOT service

MOTs provide profits for unscrupulous garages.

They fail your car for some minor 'infringement' like a tiny headlamp crack, and you pay them, the garage hopes, for a second test, plus the cost of the work.

It is cheaper to get a pre-MOT service done at the garage which is testing your car. You avoid their charges for driving your car to a test centre elsewhere first and, obviously, they will do up the car to pass first time. If you fail for a suspiciously trivial reason, check the rules with the help of your motoring rescue organisation or your local Vehicle Testing Enforcement Centre (look in the phone book), then write to the garage asking them for a refund. No joy? Report them to the local Trading Standards Officer (phone book again).

Home-made go-karts

Remember the simple pleasures of the home-made go-kart? Pram wheels on a box, steered by string reins, a plank running from front to back with a bolt at the front for the axle. I revived these for two small relatives one Christmas. Built for about £1.50 each, these vehicles won the admiration of other children.

Ask the men at your local rubbish dump to put aside a likely-looking old pram or pushchair for you when one comes in. (You'll probably have to pay them for this.) Then start work. Keep as much chassis as possible, as the tubes or plates holding the axles can be drilled through and bolted. Coach bolts, designed to hold wood to metal, are worth buying and stronger than the nails used in childhood.

Measure your child. The feet must reach the front axle with knees slightly raised, and the hips must fit the box. A good fit means better handling. Brakes are vital. Try to use those already on the pram, perhaps with an extension lever or cable pull added.

Karting is not for the fragile. You need goggles or eye-protection, helmets, gloves, even knee and elbow pads to cope with spectacular bumps. If you fear legal action, don't invite anyone else's children.

MR THRIFTY COMPUTES

Tottenham Court Road in London is a hot venue for bargain-hunters. Duty-free shops abroad, in far-flung places like Dubai, offer brilliant bargains, but you take the risk of negligible after sales service. If you intend to buy like this, allow at least an hour extra for shopping when you get to the airport. These places are as busy and noisy as cattle markets.

Half-price computers, games, electronics, cameras, music

The computer site jungle.com is linked to Software Warehouse and Telstar music and video. I have heard mixed reports of its service or lack of it; however, it offers 90,000 computer products, and countless games, CDs, tapes, vinyl records, videos and DVDs. Although it claims up to 50 per cent less than high street prices, the majority of savings are not as high: a Sony Valo laptop at £1874, against PC World's £1999.99, and current videos around £3 cheaper than HMV Shops. There is no charge for a three-day delivery; £4.99 secures next-day delivery. There is a curious £1 to £10 'insurance' fee, depending on your order cost, which protects you against loss, damage and 'any other issues relating to the delivery of the product'. In my view, these should be free to the buyer as the deliverer's insurance covers them.

If you buy software, you can automatically download it immediately. You will get loyalty points, which can be exchanged for further discounts. There is also a personal shopping service called 'my jungle' which purports to suggest future purchases to match your previous tastes, and allows you to pre-order new releases.

* 0800 0355 355 for more information.

Software to rival Windows for free, if you know what you're doing, or a very cut-price if you don't

Techies and those with time, like students, can download the Linux software system from the internet and use it for nothing. This is a rival to Microsoft, developed by Finn Linus Torvalds and 200 top programmers as a labour of love. Torvalds believes in something called 'copyleft' rather than 'copyright'; things should be free.

However, the operating manuals for Linux aren't on the internet. If you want the system with manuals, try PC World. Here, Linux Deluxe operating system costs £49.99; Windows 98, which PC World says is its 'equivalent', costs £149.99. Linux Office Suite costs £69; Microsoft Office 2000, £399. There are also games like Quake and Civilisation, but without any saving over the Microsoft versions.

* PC World, 0870 1545580

Secondhand computers and ways to get spares for outdated computers

I despise the way that computers are junked if they hiccup at six months. Computer Exchange is a chain of secondhand computer shops selling refurbished computers and hard-to-get spares for so-called obsolete kit.

You can buy, or you can swop. Stock includes Pentium III PCs, £500 (£700 new); the latest IBM DVD Thinkpad, £2400 (£3500 new); Dreamcast and Playstation consoles and games; hardware such as an Eizo 17-inch high resolution monitor, £150 (£300 new). They add that the guarantee is often better than the manufacturer's and lasts a year. Although they do not have helplines, you can phone the shop for technical help and information of any kind, or go in for a chat.

* Head office: 020 7916 1234.

Recycled toner and inkjet cartridges.

BCDS will buy empty cartridges from you, in order to recycle. It also offers good multibuy deals.

* 01935 814692.

MR THRIFTY'S FAMILY VALUES

Don't pay extra for Peter Rabbit pictures on anything!
Having a baby is a time of mad expense. New
parents don't realise they need equipment until the
last minute, then rush out and buy things in a
panic, which leads them to overspend.

Particularly, they waste huge sums on cradles,
which will only be used for a few months. Buy
secondhand or adapt a drawer. But always buy a
new mattress with safety holes in it to let the baby
breathe. Choose multi-purpose equipment, like a
baby swing that converts to a rocker and then a
high chair, and cots that become beds.

Anti-cat covers for cradles made of tiny mesh aren't
worth buying. You need one with holes the size of a
tennis net which the animal can't balance on.

Nappies
Never economise on nappies – you will just pick
up the bill in soiled Babygros – but you can do
without scented nappy disposal bags; carrier bags

are just as good. Instead of wet wipes, take a
small bottle of water and lavatory paper or
cotton wool.

Ecological disposables

Eco nappies contain a mixture of unbleached
cellulose and the water-absorbent gel in ordinary
disposables, making them 100 per cent
biodegradable. £8.50 for a 42-nappy pack; £27.95
for a 210-nappy pack from Natural Collection,
mail order, 01225 442288.

Weenees consist of a permanent waterproof pant
and a disposable inner pad which you can tear in
half and flush away. Pants cost £4.99 each; pads
cost £4.99 for 28 (small) or 20 (medium).

* Enviro UK, 3–7 Frederick Street, Luton, LU2 7QW.
01582 484899.

Simple baby toys

Make your own inverted V-shaped frame for a
tiny child to lie underneath. Suspend balloons of
various colours and sizes from a crossbar, with
string. The baby will love watching the balloons
wafting on invisible air currents, and eventually
learn how to kick them. Keep them out of reach
of growing babies.

Plastic kitchen jugs are the best bath toys.

Free toys

Anyone who looks after children can join their local authority toy library. You can take a certain number of toys out for a month. Ask your council.

Free stories

Children's libraries all have storytelling and activity sessions. Check when.

Cheap baby equipment and toys.

Nippers is a chain of equipment and toy shops which keeps prices low by operating from farms, where children can also enjoy the animals.

Branches in Hildenborough, Kent (01732 832253), Royston, Herts (01223 207071), Canterbury (01277 832008), Colchester (01787 228000), Milton Keynes (01908 504506), Rugby (01926 633100), Worcester (01386 750888), Chessington, Surrey (020 8398 3114) and Nafferton, Yorks. (01377 240689).

Information lifeline

The National Childbirth Trust has left behind its hippy image and become a must for new mothers. Membership (at local level, not the expensive national sort) gives a magazine with contacts and ideas, free teas, nanny finds and shares, and equipment for sale and hire.

* 020 8992 8637 for local contacts.

Best lavatories

When railway stations charge 20p for their toilet facilities, check the nearest Station Hotel, usually with washrooms in the basement. Large department stores are free and wonderfully equipped.

Free baby food

Write to Milupa Baby Food, Scientific Department, Milupa House, Uxbridge Road, Hayes, Middlesex, UB10 0NE (020 8573 9966) telling them your baby's birth date and they'll send samples of drinks and food for weaning a baby from four months.

Good value shoes

It is easy to get cheap children's shoes, but they will ruin their feet unless they are a proper fit. Crockers specialises in Clarks end-of-lines and slight seconds.

* N.B. Some branches are now called Clarks Factory Shops: Street, Somerset (01458 843156); Bridgwater, Somerset (01278 452617); Swindon (01793 874902); Burnham-on-Sea (01278 794668); Worle, Avon (01934 521693).

Reciprocal babysitting

You may discover through local parents that there's a babysitting circle in your area. Tokens are given according to the number of hours your children are 'sat', then you have to repay the favour. Also see my information about au pairs on page 111.

How to amuse children cheaply

For tinies, local authorities run free 'one o'clock clubs', opening slightly earlier than lunch-time with supervised indoor and outdoor areas. Older children might find adventure playgrounds nearby. IKEA stores have free, supervised 'ballrooms' where children can throw lightweight coloured balls, and a video room.

Museums and local authorities provide a gadabout existence for children during school holidays, with cheap or free activities. Look in your library for details.

For something different, plan a Theme Day. Watch the planes taking off at your local airport, free. Back home, play a game like 'What's the time, Mr Wolf?' where someone is the 'lost passenger with luggage' with their back turned on the group, who have to creep up and steal the victim's suitcase before they notice. Then give them an airline meal at home using old, chilled food containers of different sizes. Make them do the aircraft safety routine before they can eat. Come up behind their chairs and shake them a bit, then say it was turbulence.

Adapt the idea for train-lovers by buying a platform ticket. Later, have a competition for the most inventive excuse for a train's late arrival. Adapt Murder in the Dark to play Murder in the Dark on the Orient Express.

Snail races are free, and fun, and the snails don't seem to mind since they don't know they're racing.

In London, lesser-known free museums include the Bank of England, which has a brilliant bank of computers at which you can pretend to rule the world's money markets. The BT Museum is also free and full of interactive telephones, including videophones.

* All museums are now free to children. Many are also free to adults during the last hour and a half (like the Natural History Museum).

Better than a party entertainer
Your local cub scout, beaver or brownie/guide leader is probably the last repository of knowledge of how to play group games. The kind of game you play in lines passing buckets of water, string and goodness knows what. Ask them if they would, very kindly, entertain your partyload of children for an hour, either for personal payment or a donation to funds.

Hire an inflatable toy

Hire shops like HSS and others you find in *Yellow Pages* aren't only useful for heavy machinery like floor sanders; they also do a mean line in bouncy castles and, if needed, will send someone to help blow it up.

For high days and holidays, Clive and Kim Ellis hire the ultimate inflatables. A Gladiator Joust inflatable bed, with two podiums in the middle, comes complete with crash helmets and pugel sticks to push your rival onto the bed. (From £100). Bungee runs are 35-foot-long twin lanes. Competitors run as far as they can before the bungee pulls them back to base. (From £150). They also have 40-foot-long assault courses. (From £140).

* 01268 759870

Play the human juke box

For this you need people who like performing. Use the largest box you can find, and cut a TV-screen-sized square out of the front. Guests in need of entertainment should tell the jukebox what song to sing or play. S/he has to perform through the tiny TV-style hole. A hoot!

A toyshop to track down replacements

If your train set has lost or broken a vital bit, or

your child has lost some necessary bear, Arbon &
Watts can find obscure items.

* 0870 012 9090

For older children – cheap computer time.
Your local library will have computers free or for a
small fee per session. Book early, but it's always
worth turning up just in case. You can download
free games from the Internet. The following pages
are fun: www.angelfire.com (Aggahh The
Simpsons); www.winnie.qcsm.buffalo.Rdu (Mr
Edible Starchy Tuber Head Home Page – basically
potato heads); www.actionman.com;
www.co.uk.ispace.org (The Discworld Game
Pages).

Free expert help with homework online
Log on to ask a panel of 100 teachers for help with
tricky questions. Aimed at children aged 9-16.

* www.homeworkhigh.com

Exhausted?
Reverse roles. Make the children tuck you up in
bed, and read you stories. They love this. Then
you can irritate them by suddenly calling for a
drink when they have crept away thinking you are
asleep, then bounce out of bed having had a nice
little nap!

MR THRIFTY TRAVELS WISELY

Do not go away on holiday out of habit

There is a lot to be said for staying at home. It's cheaper, your bed is comfortable, the food will not upset your stomach and you do not have to get up for breakfast or leave tips for maids. Instead, adopt the old working-class habit of Going Out for Days. Short breaks of a few days have the advantage of not leaving you trying to concertina your normal week's work into the time before and after the holiday.

Consider the on-costs of any holiday

Anything needing investment in kit, like skiing, needs extra luggage to hold it; you pay extra airfreight fees and update your kit for the following year at vast expense. If you are keen on activities, find hotels which will let you hire things at reasonable rates.

If you go abroad to a malaria area, you may have to pay for vaccinations, which can add £100 to a holiday cost for a family of four. This sum will double if you go to a commercial vaccination centre rather than try your family doctor first, who will give you free many vaccinations which are charged for elsewhere.

A recent Thomas Cook survey compared costs for food and drink, for instance, once you arrive at different destinations. If you like a good dinner on holiday, consider that a meal in Florida costs three times more than a comparable meal in Corfu. A Tunisian taxi costs one-tenth the cost of one in Spain. Water skiing in Tenerife was six times as costly as in Rhodes. Poor local currencies against a strong pound also give you extra spending money, making Turkey a bargain for basics like camera film and suntan lotion.

Never buy flashy luggage

Smart luggage draws attention to you at airports, where suitcase-stealers meet the red-eye flights in the morning, pick up your cases and walk away with them while you are changing money. One solution is the bag alarm, a hook which squeals if a bag is removed.

* £17.99 (MG3254) *Innovations*, 0870 908 7070.

Buy brightly-coloured bags, which are usually discounted in shop sales because other fools are buying discreet black ones, all identical on an airport carousel. Yours will sing out, you can snatch it and be first out to the taxi rank.

I favour a zero cost packing system. Pack different types of clothing in separate supermarket carrier bags. All underpants go in one bag, all pyjamas or whatever in another, and so on. When you arrive, simply tip the contents of each bag into the drawer and hey presto! Off to enjoy yourself.

Free maps and language courses

Reserve maps at your local library before your holiday. You can also borrow language courses, though evening classes are always excellent to keep you at it, which self-taught things seldom do.

'That little place in the country we go to for weekends'

At £12 to join (or £24 family membership with up to five children included) and a fixed rate of £6.65 per night in a hostel, or £19.70 in London, it's a wonder that families don't abandon their mortgages and go and live in considerable splendour in a Youth Hostel Association mansion like King John's former castle, St Briavels, in the Forest of Dean.

There is no age limit. The atmosphere is friendly. Cars are accepted. The rooms aren't the sweaty dormitories they used to be, but clean and modern, in a trendy, minimalist way. My personal favourite is the hostel on Bristol docks, with its restaurant/art gallery.

You can book private rooms, increasingly with en suite shower rooms for no extra charge. Family rooms vary from two to six beds. Beds boast duvets, you're given your linen when you check in and, in 'refurbished' hostels, the YHA says proudly, 'carpets are guaranteed'. You don't have to scrub the kitchen in part payment, though smaller hostels might ask you to wash your plates.

Book ahead for the best places, especially for seaside hostels in Eastbourne, Brighton or the brand new Ambleside by Lake Windermere, a former Victorian hotel. For city visits, the new Liverpool International is convenient for the Albert Dock and Tate Gallery, or the converted home of one of the heroines of *Aristocrats* (the popular book and TV series), Holland House, is a stone's throw from Kensington High Street. Nostalgics will love the architecture of the former Choristers School, a stone's throw from St Paul's Cathedral. Only hostels labelled 'International' stay open all day; most hostels close in the morning and open at tea-time.

You can self-cater, or larger hostels are licensed and serve three-course meals like home-made soup, pizza and rhubarb crumble for £4.80. More adventurous hostels offer an à la carte special, such as honey and lemon glazed chicken, at £4.50 for the single dish, which means it must be quite something.

Traditionalists will be relieved to learn that you can still rough it. Black Sail Hut, at the head of Ennerdale, has gas lighting and a woodburning stove – inaccessible by car.

For even cheaper accommodation, ask about the new Camping Barns, which provide mattresses, lavatories, water and basic shelter for a group (say £60 for 16 people, sole use of a Dartmoor riverside barn) or £3.75 per person.

There are reciprocal cheap arrangements with hostels all over the world, so you can save on foreign holidays too.

* National Office, 8 St Stephen's Hill, St Albans, AL1 2DY. 0870 870 8808 for more details. Membership brings further discounts at HMV Shops, on *Lonely Planet* travel guides and a rather good 15 per cent off a cross-Channel ferry with SeaFrance.

Top drawer working holidays in lavish surroundings

The National Trust runs over four hundred conservation holidays each year at 60 historic places, for everyone aged 17–70. You could spend a weekend collecting debris from beaches and coves in Cornwall (£45 each, including accommodation), thin ancient woodlands over Christmas at Hardwick Hall or even help excavate a sixteenth-century manor house in the Chilterns, both £57.

Events volunteers spend their holiday setting up and dismantling large public events like a jazz concert with firework finale (Snowdonia) or assist at a 1940s dance at Chartwell, Sir Winston Churchill's home.

There are also naturalist holidays (Wildtrack) for those keen to get involved in nature and Working Holidays offering conservation work and the chance to abseil, canoe or whatever in supervised groups, beginners welcome.

* 020 8315 1111 for a brochure.

Romantic holidays at peppercorn prices

The Landmark Trust gives everyone a chance to stay in a giant pineapple folly, a windswept castle, or a medieval mill cottage, for peanuts. This charity restores our architectural gems and offers them for self-catering holidays at modest prices. Furnishings lack the essential naffness of so many big hotel chains, which try for the same timeless effect and miss miserably.

There are some foreign holiday lets too, especially apartments in Italy.

* Shottesbrooke, Maidenhead, Berkshire, SL6 3SW.
The Landmark Trust Handbook costs £9.50. 01628 825925.

Cheap flights

When booking air seats, it is vital to ask, before paying, when the plane leaves and returns. You often find that the cheapest fares have a catch, like a return journey at four in the morning, which they are unwilling to reveal unless you question them.

* Ryanair, 0870 156 9569; Go, BA's cheap arm, direct booking only, 0845 6054321; EasyJet, 0870 600 0000. www.easyjet.com

* lastminute.com – cheapest air seats.

* Flightbookers.com offers up to 60 per cent off scheduled flights. They promise: 'If you find a cheaper price that is available and bookable with the same airline for the same date and same route, we'll match it.'

Save money by flying as an air courier

A one-off job as an errand person. Couriers used to travel free, but charges were introduced to stop people not turning up. You don't get paid, but you get bargain air fares (perhaps half-price) and a guaranteed seat on scheduled flights. In return, you collect an envelope of documents before you fly and carry it as hand baggage to the airline desk at your destination. English-speaking staff nanny you through customs. I know someone who got her cheap fare and on the day, had nothing to carry. Couriers aren't responsible for package contents, so they can't be arrested if someone smuggles something inside.

* Try Jupiter Travel Service for Australia, 01753 689989; other services are advertised in free magazines given to Australians, New Zealanders and South Africans like *TNT* 020 7373 3377, or look in *Yellow Pages*.

Access to VIP airport lounges without paying first class ticket prices

Priority Pass is an annual ticket to airport 'executive' lounges, with their free soft and alcoholic drinks and snacks, free phones and faxes and comfy seating – even free private meeting rooms. An annual subscription of £69 gives you a list of the 266 worldwide watering-holes covered; you pay around £14 for entry to each lounge on top. Many canny business people use economy flights and this seems a good way to soften the edges of a trip, especially if you are horrendously delayed. I am unable to find a lounge which offers the shower and daybed facilities, with alarm call, that one really needs in these circumstances.

* PO Box 120, Croydon, Surrey, CR9 4NU. 020 8680 1338.

A travel agent which offers reduced rates on Concorde and the QE2

Magic Eye Breaks offers big discounts on most holiday companies' brochure prices. It also sends a series of newsletters, for the cost of a subscription, listing holidays with 'magic prices'. These are not simply last-minute bargains, but around 25 per cent off long and short haul holidays, flights and ski breaks in Europe and further afield. They seem good on cruises; I saw a 10-night QE2/Concorde break (per person) from £2295 for a double cabin to £6415 for a luxury single, compared to the list price on Concorde of £3520 and £3630 for the QE2 alone. I also noticed holidays in Barbados, Portugal, self-catering in France and a flying three-star hotel break for the Galway Oyster Festival, £249 per person for two nights. The £20 subscription cost is taken off your first holiday booking.

* Magic Breaks Ltd, L&M Business Park, Linotype House, Norman Road, Altrincham, Cheshire, WA14 4ES. 0161 929 5268.

Brand new hotels at reduced rates

'Soft openings' sound like those ready-glued envelopes, but it is the term for reduced room rates offered by new hotels while they're bedding in, so to speak.

For periods of up to three months after opening, guests are offered around a third off the normal rates not to mind if the service is eccentric (though not, I hope, like the waitress at Fowey Hall who told us to hurry up and order our breakfast so she could have hers), the TV not wired in and the gardeners are still painting the roses. This soft opening soft option extends to old hotels undergoing a facelift.

* Try the big, international hotel chains for current information such as Four Seasons, 0800 526648 and Sofitel, 020 8283 4570.

Up to 60 per cent off hotels all over the world

Resolutions is a well-established company which is a bit of a travel trade secret, used by most travel agents, but open to individuals too. It offers a computer hotel booking service with massive tentacles round the world and between 40 and 60 per cent off normal rates if you're lucky. The best times to try, they say, are the Great Rates Sales of January and February and July and August. Their service will also search for a hotel in a given place at a stipulated price, or a new hotel offering promotional rates.

* 020 8661 1983.

Don't get lost and go round the houses

You can buy pricey computerised hand-holders which tell you which road to take when you're travelling. Or consult Route 66 on a computer, and print out the results free. It will give you the shortest route, travel times and petrol costs for anywhere in Britain. Route 66 softwear at around £30 from any computer supplier and similar programs.

Free luxury hotel breaks for two at £25 a year

The Travel Offers Directory and Gold Hotel Pass
costs £23 plus £2 postage. It lists 420 hotels
throughout Britain, the Channel Islands,
Northern Ireland and Eire with comets or star
ratings after their names, at which you and a
partner can stay, free, for weeks, weekends or one
night, enjoying extras like sports facilities too.
You pay for meals, including breakfast. The book
tells you the likely cost in advance – from £11.50.
There are some stunning hotels, like the Wild
Boar, Cheshire, a gabled Tudor number ('save £76
a night' says the guide), or the castle lookalike
Skeabost House on the Isle of Skye (save £48).

* *Travel Offers Directory*, PO Box 6, Kettering, Northants, NN15
5JW. 01923 721103. www.travel-offers.co.uk

How to get compensation if you feel unfairly treated after a travel fiasco

If you are bumped from a flight because they've
overbooked, don't be fobbed off with travel
vouchers as compensation. You are legally
entitled to cash. Ask for Denied Board
Compensation. If you have any problem while
travelling, take the names and addresses of
anyone in the same situation; you have more
power as a group of complainants. The Air

Transport Users Council will take up complaints
if you have had a delayed flight and attempts at
getting compensation from your carrier have
failed.

* ATUC, 103 Kingsway, London WC2. 020 7240 6061, 2–5pm
weekdays.

Condé Nast Traveller magazine offers a free
advice and mediation service for selected cases,
as long as you have already tackled your travel
company and hit a brick wall. In some cases they
manage to get money back or ex gratia payments.

* Send photocopies of every relevant document and photographs
to: Ombudsman, Condé Nast Traveller, Vogue House, Hanover
Square, London, S1R 0AD.

Commission-free foreign exchange

If you book in advance, BAA Retail offers this at
Heathrow, Stanstead, Gatwick, Glasgow,
Edinburgh, Aberdeen and Southampton airports.
Major M&S stores also offer a commission-free
service. Thomas Cook has introduced a £2 flat fee
and is considered to have the best exchange rates.

Travel insurance

You can get free basic medical care, where this
exists in EC countries, by filling out Form E111 in
advance from the Post Office. Your extra medical

insurance in a travel policy should be £1 million in Europe and £2 million for the US. Check existing medical conditions are covered or you may have to pay a higher premium.

Try to book travel with a credit card which automatically gives you travel insurance. Before leaving, ask for a copy of the insurance policy specifying entitlements and contact numbers in case of a crisis. Take it with you, so you know what to do when the inevitable plane cancellation happens.

You can save by taking out an annual family policy – check travel sections in newspapers for good offers – but ensure that individual members of your family can use the group policy for separate trips. Asda offers family travel cover at £91.95 for a couple, with a reduction to £74.95 for single parents and no restriction on number of children.

* 0800 064 6688

Bartering rather than spending on holiday

Bartering for things is more satisfying than buying them, and you can forget exchange rates.

Show your goodies before suggesting what you want in exchange. A bottle of whisky crosses all language barriers. It is the strongest chess piece to hold, excellent for, say, getting you a room in a fully-booked hotel.

In unsophisticated countries, Marlboro cigarettes are swops for a taxi journey. Show as many packets as you mean to pay before getting in, but only hand them over after arriving safely. A plastic digital watch should secure you a day's taxi hire in Indian cities, but it goes up to a good gold watch in touristy areas.

Think about the locals' lives. If it freezes in winter, otherwise-indifferent people will jump at good warm clothes; if there are power cuts, they'll value torches and batteries, especially in Africa where they rust quickly. Jeans are always a favourite.

In places where you can't work out the coinage, little things make great tips. In Eastern Europe, they like soap, condoms and tampons – the two latter should be given discreetly. Glossy fashion magazines are great for babysitters or maids; any good newspaper for translators or more highbrow people.

Never leave beggars empty-handed, whatever travel companies say. They have so little compared to you. Rather than coins, take boiled sweets, which don't melt in the sun, and boxes and boxes of biros for children, who whoop with pleasure. They're a status symbol, and if the recipient doesn't need a biro, they can sell it.

•Wear your new clothing, rather than packing it. You will not be as upset if your luggage is lost with the new things inside.

Working and adventure holidays

Although you volunteer and work, you still pay
quite hefty sums for the privilege – up to £3000 –
with most ecological charities. Here are some
money-saving alternatives.

* Youth for Britain (01963 220036) has 250,000 gap year placements.

* Vacation Work (01865 241978) publishes handbooks such as
Summer Jobs Abroad (£9.99).

* International Voluntary Service (01206 298215) sends volunteers
to work all over the world, including Japan and Russia, for £95.

* Aquarius Worldwide (01503 262357) offers work as deckhands,
stewards and beach personnel for a £35 registration fee. You can
earn about £300 a week with tips.

Trains and coaches

From Mike Hewitson, of the Railway Users'
Consultative Committee, come the following ideas:

The National Rail Enquiry number (0345 484950) is
bound to give you 'best advice' and should know,
better than your local station, of any special offers
on your planned route. But if you have to change
lines in a major city, it is worth asking if there are
special offers on the new section of route, which
can reduce the journey price considerably.

Railcards for the under-26s and over-60s, and for

families, are worth getting if you like going on trips. Also check out local travelcards in your region. Ask about Railrovers – tickets which give you the freedom of an area or the whole country for a fixed price over a month.

Lots of discount fares are around, but don't leave it till the stated 'seven days in advance' to book; phone up months early and ask when the booking opens for those. Some tickets stipulate an outward and return train time; if you miss the train, you have to pay again. Don't forget that Saver and Supersaver tickets, which you can get on the day, insist you don't return on Fridays and some weekends.

Virgin's Trainline books any ticket for any journey in the UK, 08457 222333; www.thetrainline/co.uk offers a princely £1 off if you book over the web. For arcane savings or if in doubt, consult the *National Fares Manual* at big reference libraries.

National Express coaches offer trains a run for their money and so do smaller local coach lines. If travelling from Victoria, allow an hour to queue for a ticket; best to buy ahead through a travel agent.
*Advantage 50 Coachcard gives up to 30% National Express fares for the over 50s

* **0990 8080.**

MR THRIFTY HAS A MERRY CHRISTMAS AND A DEBT-FREE NEW YEAR

If you are shopping and feel in danger of overspending, here is my antidote. Imagine the shop stripped of all its nice decorations, not as a home-from-home but as a bare, cold warehouse. Travel forward in time to the January sales and envisage 'sale' stickers on the stock, a bit battered and piled any old way. Then would you still want to buy them? If so, wait until the Sales.

If you are socialising with families after Christmas, don't buy presents beforehand. Either recycle presents you have received, or wait until the sales.

Cheap Christmas presents

Don't beggar yourself to impress rich people. Millionaires are delighted with ordinary things they never see, like a book of stamps or a box of biros, or even this book! I've had most fan mail from the wealthy, who are fascinated by money-saving ideas. How do you think they became so rich?

A small but beautifully-wrapped gift from an expensive-seeming place is worth a large one from a cheap shop.
But if a present is funny or quirky enough, the recipient doesn't make judgements about how much it cost. Save time by buying one all-purpose wonder present, which suits all ages and personalities. Then nobody can feel favoured or hard done-by.

Try giving one lovely Christmas tree decoration. It is hard to spend over £3 on it, even at Harrods' Christmas emporium, where you then get classy wrapping for free.

Or stay at home and buy from Hawkin's Bazaar. A catalogue of cheap, eccentric and traditional toys with wonders for under £1. I love the spider's bath ladder, but my all-purpose gift is a realistic false arm and plastic hand, clad in shirt sleeve, £2.95. Add a label saying something like: 'Because you could do with a hand'. Goes down a storm used as a prop whilst singing Tom Lehrer's axe murderer's ditty, 'I hold your hand in mine dear'.

* Catalogue: 01986 782536; www.hawkin.co.uk; sales@hawkin.co.uk
Shops in Salisbury, Southampton, Tunbridge Wells, Windsor.

Other Ideas

Smells of the Forties, at 99p each, are room fresheners with a difference. Choose from U-boat (diesel fumes), Street (sweetshop toffee, cinnamon), Blitz (burning), Tea Wagon (well-stewed tea) from Eden Camp Museum, Malton, North Yorkshire, YO17 6RT. 01653 697777. 99p each; 50p p&p for one, £1 for the set.

Offer your services. Present a coupon offering to be Slave for a Morning/Afternoon/Evening. Shopping, cooking, washing, ironing, car washing and babysitting are the best gifts and cost nothing to you.

Sock Shop's brilliant sock-pairing device is a gift that can't fail. £1.95 buys a pack of five small plastic feet. You tuck your used socks into the holes in them, and they are held secure for washing and drying. 020 7329 3791 for mail order, p&p free.

Send presents in plenty of time.

Second class post is much cheaper. When doing mail order, if the item is p&p free, ask the supplier to send it direct to the recipient, so you don't have to wrap it and send it on.

Christmas decorations

Old-fashioned paper chains you stick together and hang round the room, 90p for 72 strips, Hawkin (as above), are the perfect way to occupy excited children. Cracker snaps to put inside home-made crackers, 90p for 18.

Christmas trees

Minimalist
Hang a single tree decoration where people can see it (but not steal it) along your front garden. Or instead of a tree inside, bare branches shed from trees can be put in a vase and dressed up with decorations.

Home-made
I once made an effective two-dimensional tree by cutting out a classic zigzag tree shape from cardboard, bending it in two down the middle to stand it up, and sticking on the decorations, collage style. This amuses everyone, is a great Blue-Peter-type activity for children and saves space if you live in a small place.

Cheaper trees
If you must have a real tree, go to your local city wholesale market like Covent Garden or Manchester (the best tree market in Britain) or seek local nurseries for savings and free delivery. (Don't confuse nurseries, where trees are grown, with garden centres, where they are just sold with a huge mark-up on the price; look them up in your *Yellow Pages*).

Specialist tree growers are cheapest, at from £2 a
foot, and deliver free, but only locally. Non-drop
trees are better because needles drop and can
damage your vacuum cleaner, necessitating
expensive repairs.

* The British Christmas Tree Growers' Federation can give your
nearest supplier. www.bctga.org.uk or ask Roger Hay,
0131 447 0499 (mobile, 0783 141 8886).

Cards

The simplest cards are made with gold spray
paint from Woolworths. Cut out a simple stencil
like a star or tree, lay it on the card and spray
gently round the outside.

Use clip-art, available on CD-roms cheaply from
Woolworths or Sainsbury's Savacentres. Or for
non-copyright art, try the Dover Bookshop, a
brilliant source of books you can photocopy.

* 18 Earlham Street, London WC2. 020 7836 2111. Mail order
available.

Wrapping paper

Any pink newspaper, like the *Financial Times*, or
plain brown paper purchased by the roll (not in
an expensive stationers' packet) will look good,
tied with rough string or even ends of wool.
Make a potato print, or create something on your
computer, to go on it; 'Present Circumstances

Require Further Economies' should raise a smile.

Feasts

The Quality Christmas Market Produce Farm Shop Guide is rather a long-winded name for a publication, but at least it's free if you ask for it from your local branch of the National Farmer's Union, which you'll find in *Yellow Pages*. This lists shops which will sell you a Christmas turkey by mail order.

Don't buy a big bird to cook unless you have a big family

If you buy smaller cuts of meat, you have no waste to re-offer as salad and sandwiches until they're as welcome as repeats on Christmas TV. Chicken is good value at this time of year, and exotic meat like venison can be fantastic value bought on Christmas Eve. Don't tell children they're eating Bambi!

Don't bother with a Christmas cake.

Has anyone got room for it after all that lunch?

Must have a turkey?

Buy at the last moment, advises Nicole Swengley, shopping expert at the *London Evening Standard*. 'Last Christmas, a price war developed between the major supermarkets, selling fresh turkeys for as low as 29p a pound as a loss-leader.' Frozen turkeys are cheapest, and Iceland offers the best value in these.

Alternatively, club together with others to buy turkey and other meat from Hockeys Farm, where a £75 order is delivered p&p free. This is a guaranteed BSE-free farm where animals are naturally and kindly reared. Turkey is £2.70 lb.

* South Gorley, Fordingbridge, Hants., SP6 2PW. 01425 652542 for details including of national distributors.

Good source of cheap clothes and presents
TK Maxx and Matalan are a good source of low cost designer-style clothes and presents, and TK Maxx assure me that they will be taking deliveries of bargains right up until Christmas.

* Call TK Maxx on 01707 260066, and Matalan on 01708 864350, for branches.

MR THRIFTY'S MEDICINE CHEST

Paying the chemist for medicine may be cheaper than a prescription

Before you pay the £5.90 prescription charge for your medicine, check that it doesn't cost less if you chemist sells it over the counter. Cheaper medicines include Zovirax, Piriton syrup, paracetamol tablets, Canesten cream and E45 bath oil. But check that the quantity is the same as the prescription specifies.

For a lot of prescriptions, a season ticket may work out cheaper as long as you can afford to pre-pay £30.80 for four months and £84.60 for a year. It covers all medicines issued, even if you get a different one each time.

* Form FP95, the Post Office.

All contraception is free if prescribed by a doctor or family planning clinic.

How not to catch a cold when paying for medical care

Soaring medical costs and insurance premium tax have made private health insurance expensive. Consider paying your money into a savings account instead, and then paying one-off charges for private medical care.

BUPA and Nuffield Hospitals both have fixed-price deals, at a lower cost than they charge medical insurance companies, for private payers. BUPA will quote fixed prices, inclusive of any extra days in hospital. Surgicare, a Manchester-based organisation with centres in Birmingham and London, offers fixed-price operations for hernias, varicose veins, etc., and six-month interest-free credit schemes. Ask about schemes allowing payments to be spread.

Nuffield Hospitals also offer interest-free loans for a year, provided you put down 10 per cent of the cost.

A taxi driver told me this story: a medical insurance company wrote to a friend, insured by them, asking him to pay the bill himself for an operation. They would then reimburse him, and return to him half the money saved over the price they would have had to pay the hospital, leaving him in profit.

* BUPA Hospitals, 0845 600 8822; Nuffield, 0800 688 699; PPP,0800 335 555; Surgicare, 0161 945 8688;

How to get medical insurance which does not become too expensive when you get older

Ohra (01703 620620) and the non profit-making Exeter Friendly Society (01392 477200) do not weight premiums as you get older.

How to see a specialist and have tests fast

Fast Track insurance secures early out-patient hospital appointments for people without medical insurance or with a high excess insurance policy. It doesn't offer full treatment after your audience with a medical mighty, but it will cover diagnostic testing like X-rays and blood tests. Premiums from £13 to £22.25 a month.

* Permanent Health Company, 32 Church St, Rickmansworth, Herts., WD3 1DJ. 01923 770000.

How to see a GP at home within an hour

Few of us who are self-employed, or in the private sector, or caring for children, can afford to take time off to be ill. Sick leave has become a luxury.

You can see a doctor fast at walk-in clinics near major rail stations. I was disappointed by my visit to one, where form-filling took longer than the offhand consultation by a doctor.

I know of three London-based instant doctor services; outside that area, try *Yellow Pages* under 'Doctors, Medical'.

Medical Express is a walk-in clinic at 117a Harley Street, London W1, offering consultations at £70, but £20 if you just need a repeat prescription or you know what you want. You'll have to pay the chemist the full cost of the drugs, not the NHS prescription fee, though.

* Open Monday to Friday 9–6, Saturday 9.30–2.30.
020 7499 1991.

MedCall is a 24-hour home-visiting doctor service. A GP sees you at home or your work within an hour of your call, seven days a week, for £75 (8am–6pm) or £85 outside those hours. Doctors travel as far as Kentish Town to the north, Streatham to the south, Acton to the west and the City to the east, but if they are not busy they'll go further. There is also a walk-in clinic.

* 2 Harley Street, London, W1N 1AA. 01459 131313.

DoctorCall is a similar service but wider ranging – as far as Richmond in Surrey. It offers a walk-in 24-hour service.

* 37a Lancaster Road, London, W11 1QJ. 07000 372255.

How to be seen quickly at hospital casualty

Emergency Plus is a new group of private casualty hospitals opening within the M25 area. A fixed £25 fee gives you walk-in medical attention for casualty cases or emergencies which don't need an ambulance. Emergency Plus also offers fixed-price minor surgery within ten days, e.g. £495 for simple hernias. Other services offered include fast blood tests, pathology, X-rays and sports injuries at evenings and weekends too.

* 89–93 High Road, Byfleet, Surrey, KT14 7QS. 01932 334 999 for details.

Free contact lenses for all

Contact Lens Research Consultants is an independent research group which trials new or improved contact lenses for all the major makers such as Johnson & Johnson.

They are always seeking volunteers to test lenses in clinical studies. That includes lenses for those who need bifocals, disposable or extended wear lenses and those to correct astigmatism.

All the contact lenses are provided free, together with cleaning solutions, and sometimes there is pay too – typically about £200 for 10 check-up visits.

To become a volunteer, you must be eighteen and, obviously, need to wear glasses to correct your sight. You must be prepared to visit their trials centre in Pimlico, London.

* 020 7630 9124.

Free eye examinations
If you are on income support, diabetic, suffer from Glaucoma or have a family history of this, under 16 or a student under 19, or over 60, you get a free eye examination.

Cheap replacement glasses that duplicate your favourites
It is time-consuming and expensive to choose a new pair of specs when you already have a favourite pair which has been broken or discontinued – or the favourite opticians' excuse, 'the plastic has gone too hard to put new lenses in'.

Angela Campbell Opticians offers a postal individual hand-made glasses replacement service from around £80. I found this slow, timed in weeks not days, but invaluable when my favourite reading glasses were sat on. I sent in the pieces. Back came identically shaped new frames, improved by some decoration which the makers had added for love with a note saying that if I didn't like it, send it back and they would remove it. 'We don't always make an exact copy,' Angela says. 'The guys I use are fairly resourceful. Because the frames are hand-made, they use better quality materials. Plastic frames are copied at the most reasonable costs.'

* Angela Campbell Opticians, 82 King Street, Manchester, M2 4WQ. 0161 834 7798.
E-mail manchester.branch@angelacampbell.co.uk

Free access to newly-developed drugs, and payment for taking them

International Clinical Trials is a company which tests new drugs before they go on sale. It uses, on the whole, healthy people aged between 18 and 45, but is always looking for people over 65, to try new drugs. When I spoke to them, they were trying out a new anti-depressant. They paid their human guinea-pigs £50 per visit to visit their Central London test centre weekly for nine weeks. Or contact your local hospital.

If you have a specific medical condition, you can ask to go on their lists in case a drug to treat this appears, and then you can get access to (possibly) cutting-edge treatments not yet generally available. On the downside, any new drug may give you headaches, nausea or other unpleasant symptoms. In very rare cases, it has more serious effects, e.g. on your liver, in which case the trial is stopped immediately.

* 0808 100 1177 between 8am and 7pm, weekdays.

Free dental treatment

Gnash your teeth at rising dentistry costs by getting
free treatment, including false teeth, from dental
students at any major teaching hospital. You must
de-register at your ordinary dentist and register at
the hospital during weekday working hours. If
you're in pain, they will treat you immediately and
give you regular check ups. The snag is that each
stage of the work is checked, so a five-minute filling
can take an hour. For complicated work, you may
have to wait six months. But you can save
hundreds of pounds.

*** For your nearest teaching hospital, phone the British Dental
Association, 020 7935 0875.**

Free homeopathy

Homeopaths can overcharge outrageously. But you
can get effective homeopathic treatment, and any
number of alternative therapies including
osteopathy, free on the National Health Service.
Simply ask your GP to refer you. If s/he won't,
change your doctor or refer to your local
Community Health Council or MP.

The Royal London Homeopathic Hospital has staff
fully qualified in conventional medicine who treat
26,000 out-patients a year and 700 in-patients with
all mainstream medical techniques and drugs plus
complementary therapies like Iscador therapy
(mistletoe extract) for cancer sufferers, acupuncture
and osteopathy. Prescriptions are dispensed just as

with ordinary drugs; you don't pay if you're exempt.

* Great Ormond Street, London, WC1N 3HR. 020 7833 7276 for appointments.

* The Homeopathic Hospital, Tunbridge Wells, is another good centre treating out-patients only. Church Road, Tunbridge Wells Kent TN1 1JU. 01892 542977.

* For a free list of homeopaths in your area, send an SAE to the British Homeopathic Association, 27a Devonshire Street, London, W1N 1RU. 020 7935 2163.

Cheap vitamins

Healthspan Direct is a Guernsey-based mail-order service claiming to offer vitamins and health supplements 'at tax-free prices' and p&p free. They say the important thing, when evaluating value, is to check the strength of ingredients in each tablet. They always state this. High strength 570mg cod liver oil is £7.95 for 360 capsules, a year's supply.

* PO Box 64, Guernsey, GY1 3BT. 0800 731 2377.

MR THRIFTY SAVES ON HEATING, LIGHTING, WATER AND POWER

Hot water is a serious drain on your bank balance. Showers are cheaper, but Power Showers cost as much as baths. Electric heaters, especially fans, burn money. Substitute a portable Dimplex-style oil radiator which stays warmer for longer once turned off.

If you can't afford to heat your bedroom, electric blankets are good warmers. A double blanket, which you pre-heat and turn off, uses half the power of an overblanket. Cheaper still is an old-fashioned hot water bottle substitute: a warm stone or brick. You pop this into your oven or fire (which you're already using) to get hot, then wrap it in a blanket and transfer it to your bed.

According to the Energy Savings Trust, the average household can save £278 a year on heating by increasing loft insulation to at least eight inches; installing cavity wall insulation, if your house is post-1930; renewing older boilers (an expensive condensing boiler saves 30 per cent of electricity); adding heating controls to the central heating system (and turning the heating down a few degrees); and switching to energy-saving lightbulbs (The Natural Collection catalogue has a selection and gives individually-tailored recommendations, 01225 442288).

There are old-fashioned ways of saving heating. You lose around nine per cent of your heating through doors and windows. Hanging a thicker or interlined set of winter curtains cuts draughts. I have had my main curtains made with a hook-in lining for winter. You can also buy foam draught excluder strips for the bottom of doors and windows, or stuff a stocking to make a doorstop. Warning – don't make a room too airtight.

Free advice and information about grants
Ask the Energy Efficiency Hotline for a free Home Energy Check questionnaire, a ticklist about your number of rooms, etc., which enables the Hotline to suggest ways you can save. It will also explain how to get a grant of £200 towards home improvements like condensing boilers or loft insulation. If you have one improvement, you can still get money for a second one. You must contact them before you begin the work, as they stipulate the suppliers you must use.

* 0345 277200.

You need a real fire against serious damp

Electricity is, in my experience, useless against damp. I once lived in a houseboat so damp that my clothes rotted in the wardrobe, until I found an old cast iron coal-burning stove, a former railway waiting-room heater called The Celebrated Bogey. One coal fire each night kept the place warm and dry all day, and I cooked food in its small oven and boiled a kettle on top.

* Architectural salvage dealers like Architectural Heritage, The Woodyard, A5 Brockhall, Weedon, Northants., NN7 4LB (01327 349249) can provide restored ranges; also try Rod Hughes, 01260 227641; best advice for modern stoves is from Croydon Fireplaces, 2 Campbell Road, Croydon, Surrey. 020 8684 1495.

Change your supply company, cut your bills

If you pay your bill by direct debit, or monthly fixed rate, you will find your fuel prices cheaper.

But you can change to any supply company in the country without having new cabling or pipework, saving at least £20 a year on a £260 electricity bill alone. Before switching, ask a potential new supplier whether they charge different rates for different times of the day. If you are offered a fixed time contract, say for a year, ask whether it has penalties for ending it early.

You might save by handing both your gas and electricity supplies to one company, like British

Gas (0345 400200), which offers a cheap deal for both, although then you are in the hands of a company whose service has its critics, let's say. Worth looking at is newcomer Independent Energy (0800 1951995) which emerged consistently cheapest by around £20 in a *Daily Mail* region-by-region survey in August 1999. If over 50, also check Saga Energy for around £50 off a typical gas bill.

But you might save more, overall, by first going to a comparison service which takes your annual fuel bills and calculates the best deal for you.

* OFGEM (0800 887777) supplies a full list of gas and electricity suppliers, OFFER (0800 451 451) will send you free leaflets listing the prices of every electricity supplier.

* Several websites offer to calculate, free, whose service will save you money if you supply the figures you paid last year. www.kura.co.uk says a recent survey showed that a typical customer saves £89 a year when they switch suppliers. www.buy.co.uk and www.nfcg.org.uk are other examples.

Sideways savings

Barclaycard has links with Eastern Energy (0800 7313313) to offer up to 13 per cent off your bill if you pay with the card. Norweb (0800 195 2953) customers receive Tesco Clubcard points for their fuel bills and Page & Moy holiday discounts. Goldfish card customers receive up to £75 off Centrica bills. Scottish Hydro (0800 300000) offers Air Miles. David Crombie tells me that Seeboard's thank you card is free to its customers and offers 'free energy units' from time to time, and discounts on meals, cleaning and holidays in its National Savings Guide.

* 0800 068 0681

Interest-free central heating
Always install new fires, boilers, central heating systems, new water tanks and that kind of thing in the summer. This is the slow period and you can always find offers and interest-free credit.

However, very big companies often sub-contract work out to independent plumbers. Ask them how much it would cost for a quote without going through the big company. Although you won't get interest-free credit, this will result in savings all the year because the big company will add a mark-up to recover the cost of the interest-free credit, and the small guy won't.

I had my boiler installed by an independent plumber whom I knew, and who also offered me a personal faults repair service at considerably less than the British Gas equivalent. This only works if you trust a plumber, and are assured that his plumber brother, whom you also know, will fill in for emergencies if plumber number one is away. It becomes interesting when the brother is not told of this arrangement and you call him.

How to buy energy-saving appliances

Before you buy any gas or electrical kitchen machine, look for the rainbow label on the side. This is an EC efficiency rating.

The bright green A-rating means the machine is very efficient; a machine with a red G-rating will cost you most on operating costs. According to official figures, if you bought a B-rated fridge freezer instead of an E-rated one, you save £15 on electricity per year.

It's worth looking for water consumption figures, especially if you have a water meter. A washing machine using 60 litres per wash rather than the standard 80 will save you 5800 litres a year. The labels, however, aren't easy to read. The Energy Efficiency Hotline may be able to translate. 0345 277 200.

How to save power on cooking

A multi-tiered saucepan will allow you to cook all stages of your meal on one cooker ring. Lakeland sells a veritable tower of bubble (five multi-tiered steamer, £99, 01539 488100) and cheaper variations, or look in camping shops for stacked tiffin-carrier-type pans for pence.

Never use saucepans in materials which heat up slowly, like cast iron, for quick-cooking things like fried eggs; you will waste heat and have a long wait while it gets hot. Then after using it for a few minutes, you have a pan all heated up with nowhere to go, so to speak. But you can save fuel if, say, you have a lot of bacon to fry for breakfast, by turning the fuel off beneath a cast iron pan once it is fully hot. It will use residual heat to cook the rest.

If you use the oven, fill it fully. Even children's oven chips and fish fingers can be baked, rather than grilled, while you cook your own casserole on another tray. Think ahead: cook two days' meals in one, then you can re-adopt our grandmothers' thrifty techniques, like only having hot food on alternate days or putting hot food or even a pot of tea or coffee in vacuum flasks to keep warm for later. Once used, leave the oven door open as a way of giving your kitchen extra heat in cold weather.

Microwave ovens make a magical electrical saving. A Christmas pudding takes several hours on a cooker, but two minutes by microwave. They also save washing up, and hot water, because they are convenient for anything sticky, which gets burnt-in in a conventional saucepan. Rice, potatoes, scrambled eggs and porridge slide smoothly from a microwave container, and you can make custard in its serving jug and hot chocolate in its mug, as long as you are careful about over-hot handles.

You don't need expensive special microwave cooking apparatus, just china pudding bowls (I save mine every Christmas from puddings) and thick plastic containers like Vitalite margarine tubs, whose sturdy lids save the need for clingfilm over whatever you are cooking.

When buying a microwave, complex computerised thingies add hundreds to the price. Unless you are prepared to puzzle through the instructions, go for a simple oven. You need at least 650 watts of power; beware of cheap deals that don't offer at least this, and a timer for at least half an hour.

No-fuel cooking

Mike and Tessa McKirdy of Cook's Books, Rottingdean gave me a book called *The Housewife's ABC* (1921) which told me about haybox cooking. This is a slow cooking method which takes three hours to cook what a powered cooker will do in one, but it is free.

Take a wooden box with a tightish lid, or a tin trunk. Line the base and the lid with several layers of newspaper. Half-fill with hay, or hay and wood shavings, or those little pellets of polystyrene we get as parcel packing. Choose casserole dishes, preferably earthenware, with tight-fitting lids so steam doesn't evaporate. Put the box close to the cooker and transfer the pans into it so you don't lose heat in carrying them around. In the box, leave enough space for a cushion on top. Pack more hay tightly round, keeping each dish three inches from the next. When the hay is nearly level with the top, cover with the cushion. Put the box away from cold floors and draughts. This haybox doubles as a fridge in summer: cold pots will stay that way and it is fly-proof.

A haybox dinner party is a piquant idea and it means all your cooking is done hours early. A haybox won't boil food, but it will keep it warm and gently cook porridge, casseroles, stews and vegetables started off in the conventional cooker. You can even make jam with it, provided the first skimming is done before you put the pan in the box, and you need less sugar.

Candles and oil lamps

I would like to recommend hand-wound torches as alternative sources of power, but they run down too quickly. Candles are a good alternative to electric light, behind glass for safety. Use only plain white; coloured ones smoke and leave marks. Make candles last longer by dipping the outsides in varnish to stop wax running down the sides (hold them by the wick and dip them in a can, but don't varnish the wick).

Improvise an oil lamp using cooking oil and a hefty cork as used in storage jars, with a piece of cotton string through the middle, an inch at the top and bottom as a wick. Fill a glass two-thirds full of water, then slowly pour cooking oil on top to make a layer an inch deep. Carefully float the cork on top, allow the wick to absorb some oil, and light.

Savings on water

Water companies make much of water meters. Usually only single people save money with a meter, but for a rough idea of the figures, your local water company will be able to use its ready reckoner system to tell you. I should be wary. If asked odd questions, like whether you've had lots of home improvements done recently, go quiet. They are probably leading up to forcing you to have a water meter. It's the rules, you see.

If forced to have a water meter, ask for the free 'water hippo' which you put in your lavatory cistern to save water used on the flush.

From 1 April 2000 there is no installation fee for water meters. Most water companies will offer you a gamble: if your metered bill is more expensive than your previous fixed charge, you can send the meter back after a year. Of course, they won't refund the difference in your bill.

If you have a water butt in your garden, which catches rainwater for use, some companies offer money off your water bill. They are reluctant to admit this but it is true, so persist.

If desperate, move to a cheaper area!

The fixed water charge is based on how big your house is, and how expensive an area you live in. Houses in higher council tax areas will, unfairly, pay more.

Free pipe repairs

Generally, you're responsible for leaking pipes in your house. But all the water companies (except Mid-Kent Water) will repair leaking pipes in your garden for free. That doesn't apply if your pipes are in an appalling state of repair and will need complete replacements because they're likely to spring a leak elsewhere in your herbaceous border. It is the same with gas.

Savings on a swimming pool in your garden

If you install a swimming pool in your garden, you will find yourself liable for extra water charges. You can have a pool-style experience at considerable saving if you buy one of the new inflatable family-sized paddling pools.

OFWAT, the water company regulatory body, tells me that if the water company find out, they might, just might, slap a charge on you for 'leisure' use of water. It's up to you to decide how tell-tale your neighbours are. With a blow-up pool, you don't have to pay for its cleaning or construction, and you can deflate it and reclaim your lawn when a heatwave ends.

* For a super paddling pool, try Argos Direct, 0870 600 2020.

Saving money by taking the mineral build-up out of your pipes and appliances

Electronic descaling systems clip on to your water pipe to send an electronic pulse through the water which eliminates hard water and removes limescale which encrusts pipes and elements. Scalewatcher claims to save up to £190 in extra energy and maintenance costs.

* Fast Systems Ltd, Freepost, Henley-on-Thames, Oxon., RG9 1ZZ. 0500 001109.

Saving money on big home housework machines

If your washing machine, tumble dryer, dishwasher, fridge, freezer, video or TV is on its last legs, don't buy a new one. DER Direct offers Whirlpool home appliances to rent from £10.99 a month. Delivery, installation, and all servicing are free, and if the machine can't be fixed they offer a free replacement, with a guarantee of no price increase. You have to agree to rent for 18 months, or you can get out of your agreement earlier by giving 28 days' written notice.

If you share a house, have a large family or don't have money to spend upfront, try DER Direct's coin-in-the-slot machines to rent. You must pay a £15 administration fee to start. Then they install a washing machine, or whatever, which costs £1 per wash in the slot meter. This meter is emptied each month, the £20.50 rent and damage insurance taken, and the rest is refunded to you.

* 0800 625 625.

Buying kitchen appliances and keeping them going

The back of any magazine about smart homes will give you lots of discount kitchen appliance sellers. People recommend Buyers and Sellers, 020 7229 1947. Also try COD Electrical, 0161 941 2471 and Tempo stores, 020 8547 0404. My favourite is Hot and Cold Inc., 020 8960 1200, for their generosity. They have been known to give a machine a swift kick at the back and say: 'It's dented, take a discount.' Also look at catalogues like *Freemans* (0800 900 200) which give you a 10 per cent 'commission', i.e. discount, worth having on a big buy.

Reconditioned machines (like Agas) bought from dealers are better than secondhand ones bought from individuals; you get a guarantee that it's in working order.

Taking service records into account before buying

Resist buying appliances from a fitted kitchen firm. If they break down, you have to contact the firm to activate the guarantee and they may not want to know.

Cut the need for repairs by buying as few machines as possible and those less likely to break. A *Which?* magazine survey listed washer-dryers as most prone to prang.

There is no overall Most Breakable Make, but the least reliable names in another *Which?* magazine survey were Hoover, Hotpoint and Servis for washing machines; Zanussi for fridge-freezers; Tricity-Bendix for microwave ovens; and Ferguson for TVs and video recorders. Only Miele rose above average, but they are pricey.

Some manufacturers' service lines are always engaged. During my three days' research, in which I posed as a customer needing repairs, I couldn't contact Electrolux, Bosch, Siemens, Gaggenau and Neff. If a repairs department is always engaged, use the ringback service, pressing 5 and putting the phone down. It tries for 45 minutes and costs about 10p.

A repair service

Norwich Union Direct's Ultimate Appliance Breakdown Cover is a no-quibble service for all major home machines under eight years old, including your hi-fi and video recorder. They pay in full or will replace faulty machines sometimes. From £12 a month. 0800 888223.

There will always be a corner of my heart for the woman who was taken to court because she locked a boiler service engineer into her kitchen rather than let him go away to get yet another spare part.

MR THRIFTY, MAN OF LETTERS

Recycled envelopes

I rarely use new envelopes, and never buy new wadded envelopes like Jiffy bags, which cost 35p or more. I heard of a man who actually turns his envelopes inside out to re-use them, by separating them where they are glued, which is a bit long-winded. Don't bother to buy special labels to stick over old addresses; simply strike through the old address and stamp and write the new one.

Don't forget the good old strategy of steaming unfranked stamps off envelopes with a kettle.

Paper

For some years I shared a house with three writers. Paper was always in viciously short supply. As a result, I write on both sides of paper as a matter of course.

For documents, I use boxes of old paper, begged from printers and those new high street print shops, because it contains a mistake or is simply surplus to requirements – more common now that phone codes are always changing. If you are faxing someone, use the blank side. They need never know that the other side of your paper contains some alien logo or slogan.

Saving postage and phone bills
Send things by fax. If you don't have a fax machine, and can't ask a friend who may have access, ask a library or local newsagent, or even a local small business. It shouldn't cost more than 5p a page.

Saving stamps by knowing what to ask for
Don't waste money by asking for Registered Post when Recorded Delivery or even just a free Proof of Postage certificate would do.

Recorded delivery means the thing is tracked for safety. Special Delivery ensures your letter or package gets to where it's supposed to before noon next day and insures the contents against loss or damage up to £250 for £3.35. This cost increases for higher insurance, up to £2500. If its non-arrival means 'consequential loss' for you – say you are bidding for a contract and would lose out of your bid isn't delivered on time – you can pay extra to insure against your loss, from £1.20 (£1000 loss) to £2.50 (£7500 loss). Don't bother to send things Special Delivery on Friday as the Post Office won't deliver on Saturdays, if next day delivery is your principal objective; use a delivery firm. I find Londonlink cheapest, at £5.95 (plus VAT) upwards for a 24-hour delivery.

* 020 8889 8899

I have come across post office officials who refuse to despatch anything by any special service without a full postcode on it.

Money off parcels sent abroad

From Michael Honychurch comes this tip to save money on parcels sent abroad. The parcel must weigh 2kg or less.

Write 'SMALL PACKET' on the outside. On the largest parcel you save nearly £3 on the regular fee of £18.15. Be prepared to fill out a customs declaration. You can enclose 'personal correspondence relating to what's inside' like a Happy Birthday note, but not screeds of paper. You have to point out that this is going at the small packet rate to get the savings. Even the best-willed clerks don't know all the rules.

Money-off stationery

Quill is a stationery catalogue full of 'penny pinchers': its own brand sticky message pads at 12p per dozen, and computer peripherals at eye-openingly cheap prices. Free next-day delivery on orders above £30, drivers who will carry and set up heavy things, and rather good freebies with the first order.

* PO Box 7629, Birmingham, B19 3RQ. 0800 496 0644 for a catalogue.

Office World has 24 national superstores with a mail-order catalogue which claims that if you find cheaper, they will refund twice the price difference.

* 0345 444700 for a catalogue or nearest store address.

Staples sells a pen for 10p and says that it will match any cheaper price, and give the finder half the difference again.

* 0800 141414. staples.co.uk

MR THRIFTY USES THE TELEPHONE

Unless you're in business, or away all the time, you don't have to shackle yourself to the bleeping tyranny of an answerphone. If it's important, people will call back or send a letter.

BT's discounts
Complex. You need help to work through these and so do BT's staff. Look up bt.com on the internet for the latest, then ask and persist. Dial 150 for the Sales Department.

All BT customers get a free 10 per cent discount on 10 nominated Friends and Family numbers, including one international and one mobile number. From these, you can nominate a BestFriend for 20 per cent off.

If you dial abroad a lot, you can add five Friends and Family Overseas extra numbers for 10 per cent off for £1 a quarter.

If you spend over £25 a quarter including VAT, get a free discount.

Join Call and Save free. It gives you 10 per cent off calls, with Friends and Family discounts on top. There is a second scheme, Option 15, costing £4 a quarter and offering 10 per cent off all calls too, but I can't see the point of it.

If you spend over £70, pay for a discount

Subscribe to PremierLine at £6 a quarter to get 15 per cent off (5 per cent off mobile and premium rate calls), with Friends and Family discount making that 25 per cent, or 15 Friends and Family Overseas numbers.

On top of that, get another 10 per cent off all daytime calls for 50p.

For home workers, Daytime Caller, at 50p a month, gives you 10 per cent off national and regional daytime calls made between 8am and 6pm. Team this with Friends and Family to make 19 per cent, 23.5 per cent with PremierLine and 32.5 per cent with both.

If you have a second line, get the calls half-price.

BT Together costs £11.99 a month (for new or existing second lines) and gives you half-price on 'some of your phone calls'. Check what that means; BT didn't know. But you can't have PremierLine and things like that too.

25 per cent off international calls without hassle

Country Calling Plans are for people who habitually call a particular country. £1 per month gives 25 per cent off calls to your stipulated country. (See later in this chapter for deals offered by some of the other telephone operators).

Getting money back on the bill

If you get a wrong number and you didn't misdial, call the Operator (100) and ask for a credit on your phone bill. This service also works if you are given the wrong number by Directory Enquiries.

Impartial advice on buying a mobile phone

You can buy a mobile phone and pay for your calls (that's called subscription). Or you can pay a monthly charge with a set number of minutes 'free' within the rental, or even unlimited phone time (all-inclusive).

Or you can buy a 'prepay' phone in a box, with top-up vouchers to cover the cost of calls, from newsagents or electronics shops. Check what you're buying. A friend who let her vouchers lapse found her phone cut off without the option of restarting it.

Try to buy a mobile which does not charge for retrieving messages. If you are being charged 8p per minute for this service, leave a message on the mobile's answerphone telling callers to leave a message on your landline at home, unless it's life and death.

Get insurance cover if you break or lose a phone, which gives you an immediate replacement, rather than heartbreakingly long waits or a hugely priced new phone.

The Carphone Warehouse has a 110 per cent money back promise that you can't buy lower. Its *What Tariff?* guide lists its top five in each category of phone, subscription, all-inclusive and prepay. BT Cellnet and Vodafone top each category. The shops also have in-house repair people and an Express Repair Desk offering a two-hour repair (020 8896 5065 for locations). If you haven't got insurance, ask whether they will loan you a replacement phone while you wait, which they should do if they have one. A good compromise, if you don't want the extra cost of owning a mobile, may be to hire one for short-term use or even a night. 020 8896 5050.

* Customer care, 020 8896 5096; if you don't want to go to the shop, the direct sales line, which delivers next day, is 0800 424 800.

* The PocketPhone Shop (0800 102102) has a free, easy to understand *Guide to Tariffs* listing every option with its pros and cons. I found this an unpressured place.

Free phone line and reduced bills.
Cable and Wireless offers a free phone line with its £9.99 monthly subscription to its cable TV, and 100

free minutes of local evening calls. Worth looking at, but some I know have found the company hard to contact when they needed repairs.

* 0800 068 7899.

A cheap and simple mobile deal

Virgin Mobile has no charges other than calls – 15p per minute for the first ten minutes of use, then 10p per minute for the next ten minutes; then 5p per minute even at peak rate. You don't have to stay in continuous credit and can top up your phone-time free by credit card or scratchcards bought from petrol stations; A Startpack costs £12.50 including £10 worth of calls. Users can claim Xtras – other deals including 10% off holidays.

* 0845 6000 600 or 6000 789

How to save on phone calls abroad

Try using your mobile phone. My Orange phone deliberately undercuts BT's international calls substantially.

Or get a computer and learn how to e-mail. For the price of a local call, you can 'chat' (by typing) for as long as you like to people overseas. Don't actually write your messages whilst connected. You pre-prepare them, then send them in a few seconds over what is called a Flashsession.

Or join the various cheap-time services. These can give you half-price calls, mainly by re-routing your calls through cheaper telephone services, usually in America, with no VAT and many free calls. You can find many 'pay as you go' international phone services by asking a newsagent, who will sell you a pre-payment card. Otherwise, check deals in the travel or money section of your newspaper. Most of these involve paying a deposit, for which you can give your credit card, and which will be taken off your bill. You are given a personal number. You dial them, dial in your identity number, and dial your desired number.

The best I have found is WorldxChange Communications, which does not take a deposit nor require you to remember a PIN number. You just register and dial 1861 before each number you call, in Britain and abroad.

* 1 Exchange Tower, Harbour Exchange Square, London, E14 9GB. 0800 294 0000.

Never use a hotel phone to dial out

You will be charged horrendously. Ordinary phonecards used in public phones are also more expensive than mobile phones. If you don't want to take your mobile phone, get a BT Chargecard or similar card from American Express. You key in your personal code before making a call, and the cost is put on your home bill.

Saving the directory enquiries fee

It annoys me that main Post Offices no longer have banks of national telephone books giving you numbers free. Directory enquiries are free from public telephone booths. You are entitled to two (not one) phone numbers for your fee so save up enquiries if dialling at home!

Free Internet membership

To get on the worldwide web, you need an Internet service provider. They are your link, and you can pay a monthly fee of around £8, which should give you a fast service and phone helpline. Or you can pay nothing. However some services make money by charging heftily for helplines – £1 a minute sometimes. So find a provider who offers all the necessary set-up programs on a CD-rom without needing you to phone in.

Some free service providers are slow to connect, costing you phone time – the worst I found in a survey took over 14 minutes. A BBC Watchdog report lists Tesconet (0345 225533) as one of the best, also giving you ten free e-mail addresses to cover all family members. Virgin Net (0845 600 0600) is another efficient free service. Also try the oldest freebie service, Freeserve, provided by Dixons (0870 9090666) Or Free-Internet (0800 9801 666).

Put your Internet service provider on your BT Friends and Family list to get discounts on phone time.

MR THRIFTY SAVES TIME, MONEY AND TEMPER

A free guide to your legal rights to wave around in shops

Machines have characters, like pets and people. Usually the most attractive are irredeemably faulty and resist all repair. If you buy a bad 'un, refuse the shop's offer of free repairs. This is entering a circle of hell in which you have legally 'accepted' the machine and can't claim your money back later when it goes wrong for the umpteenth time. Instead, ask for your money back at once, or an exchange. Not a credit note, which you can't exchange for money later.

These are your legal rights, and you will find more of this useful stuff in a booklet from the Department of Fair Trading called *A Shopper's Guide*. Among other useful facts are that notices claiming 'no refund on sale goods' are illegal.

* *A Buyer's Guide* (printed or cassette form) and all sorts of leaflets on your rights when buying home improvements, a used car, using an estate agent to sell your home, buying shoes, by post, prepaying, being refused credit, buying goods or a service (with separate leaflets for Scotland and Northern Ireland), using a pawnbroker and credit, in Welsh where appropriate, are available from: OFT, PO Box 366, Hayes, UB3 1XB. 0870 60 60 321. E-mail: oft@echristian.co.uk; website: www.oft.gov.uk

Complaining: I share my secrets

I would like to complain that it's necessary, these days, to complain. If you don't, you might as well throw your money to the four winds, because few people in companies seem to concentrate on the simplest transactions and do them right the first time. Some days, I have saved more money by complaining than I have earned in a week.

Because, whatever the law, big companies are like noblemen's private armies and play to their own rules. 'The insolence of office' Shakespeare called it and he never wrote truer words. The standards of maturity, of training, of knowledge about what a company offers, and of sheer kindness and humanity, are sadly lacking in invisible phone-answering 'customer service advisers' or whatever daft titles they hide behind.

Get the names of the people on the phone as you go along. They will behave better if they know they can be traced. For this reason, they deliberately mumble their christian names, and when challenged, insultingly saying it's company policy to protect against 'intrusion'. Balderdash! Answer that they have your details on their screen and they must give you theirs.

You only have to get one silly person on the phone, who slams the phone down when s/he feels you have been 'rude' (i.e. being tiresome to them by disagreeing with their version of events), to ruin your day and cost you precious minutes redialling, then giving your postcode and your maiden aunt's name or whatever their security requirement is. So, if they're rude, use it as ammunition to extract even more.

Work out whether it's worth complaining first, though. What, realistically, do you want to happen as a result of your complaint? State this, when you find someone half-sensible to talk to about it. 'I want this changed/I want this person re-trained/I just want someone to say sorry/I want £800 recredited to my account' or whatever. I have said all these things on the phone when complaining, and that's just in the last few months, not years.

People say you shouldn't digress, adding in other complaints, but should stick to your point. Personally, I embroider my complaint as much as possible, making it so florid and often personal and full of dark emotion, crisis and emergency, that it seeps into the cracks between the hard rock that makes up most of a customer service person's brain. This is a trait I observed in my late mother, who could make strong workmen cry at 50 paces and unfortunately also used it to win any party game, no matter how trivial.

Persist. If you hit a brick wall when complaining, finish the conversation quickly. Then dial in again to get a new and more pliant 'customer service operative'. Or ask for the next person up in the chain of command. They always have more authority to grant you the thing you want.

Lose your temper if you must. Use the 'you hold him, I'll hit him' principle: be aggressive to one person, then, when they put you through to the next person whispering 'He's a nightmare', be charm incarnate and say things like: 'I know you can help me, I just felt we were going round in circles because your colleague did not grasp my point'.

If you don't succeed, go right to the top. Managing Directors hate getting calls of complaint. In a dire state? Seek the help of your local Trading Standards Officer or the free legal advice line usually offered by your house insurance, union or club.

Finally, when you receive your refund and a big bouquet, phone and thank the sender charmingly. They will be so surprised that the emotional impact of your complaint will come home to them. You have shown what a charming person you are. It will make them wake at night, sweating and questioning their company!

A good long-term result of making an effective complaint, and being charming about it when you have got your own way, is that you end up with an address book full of the direct lines of senior officers willing to take up your cause in the future or even pay in cheques for you in their lunch hour (yes, it has happened). 'May I *always* phone you from now on?' you may purr. 'You seem to understand my needs as a customer so well.' They will be putty in your hands.

Some companies wear you out by putting you on hold and playing awful music at you until you give up. If you can't reach a real person on a switchboard customer services number, look up the company's ordinary non-0800 number in the business phone book, and dial them. Explain your problem and say: 'I feel sure there is another number you know to get through to them on' and, magically, you'll be told it.

Paying bills without spending more
Don't pay bills by post and waste envelopes and stamps. Pay by direct debit, free, at your bank. You can also pay some bills, like gas, free at your Post Office or through Internet banking systems – if you can master them.

Check your bills carefully
A friend who took a temporary job in the

accounts department of a large store told me this story. A man bought a £600 saddle on account. The computer mangled the paperwork, losing his name and account number. 'Don't worry, we never lose out,' said my friend's boss. He added £600 to the bill of every account customer who shopped in the department regularly – perhaps two hundred people. Only a quarter queried it. The rest just paid.

Querying bills is free and should never be embarrassing. 'Just checking!' you say breezily.

Query silly bills

Professionals who should know better still send amateurishly vague and huge bills. Query them. I successfully refused to pay a surgeon several hundred pounds for a bad operation.

Ask the bill-sender to 'reconsider', a word with a gentlemanly tone which allows him or her to withdraw with dignity intact. Ask for an itemised breakdown and, if you don't agree, say so, giving reasons. Many professionals belong to organisations with strict rules, and a client arguing through the formal procedures is a time-consuming hassle which they could do without. So if you have a reasonable objection, or they don't want to lose you, they will usually adjust the bill.

Places to complain to

Ombudsmen. Free, and to be consulted before lawyers because once a complaint is in a lawyer's hands the ombudsman won't act.

These official regulators can look into misbehaviour by financial institutions and local authorities and force them to 'review their position'. Complaining is free; send clear copies of all correspondence.

- Banking: David Thomas. 020 7404 9944.
- Building Societies: Josephine Thompson. 020 7931 0044.
- Investments: (Peps, Isas, Unit Trusts). Peter Dean. 020 7796 3065.
- Insurance: Laurie Slade. 020 7902 8100.
- Personal Investment Authority (Investments): Tony Holland. 020 7216 0016.
- Personal Insurance Arbitration Scheme: (Disputes about insurance policies). 020 7837 4483.
- Securities and Futures Authority Complaints Bureau: 020 7676 0912.
- Pensions: Julian Farrand. 020 7834 9144.
- Estate Agents: Stephen Carr-Smith. 01722 333 306.

For others, like the Local Authorities Ombudsman, check *Yellow Pages*.

For cases of financial abuse by public or quasi-public organisations or officials, try the National Audit Office. This brilliant bunch of people are

fearless in their criticism of skulduggery and
goings-on.

* 157 Buckingham Palace Road, London SW1. 020 7798 7000.

Journalists
Newspapers spearhead our proud tradition of
free speech and they're your best line of defence
against injustice, if you can find a journalist who
will listen to your story. The *News of the World*
and the *Sunday Times* do excellent investigative
work. Most newspaper Money sections have
problem pages to try to sort out personal cases of
dodgy dealing, especially with banks and
building societies. 'Jessica Investigates' in the
Saturday Telegraph is good; Roger Anderson in the
Mail on Sunday is another.

Going to law
To be avoided. Citizens' Advice Bureaux and
sometimes Local Authority Law Centres give free
legal advice if you hit a snag in life. Most house
insurance policies include a free legal advice
helpline to give you brief opinion on how to
handle most thorny problems. If not, does your
union or any organisation of which you're a
member offer legal help?

* The Consumers Association has a legal advice service costing
£9.35 to members, £12.75 to non-members quarterly. If they take

a case further than simply talking on the phone, and have to write a letter, the average cost is £250. 0800 252 100.

* The Accident Line is a free service backed by the British Medical Association offering 30 minutes' free advice to accident victims about compensation from specialist solicitors. 0500 192939.

* Lawyers for your Business otganise 30 minutes' free advice if you're setting up a business. 020 7405 9075.

No-win-no-fee solicitors advertise in newspapers and on TV. For most people who can't pay £100 an hour for a solicitor, this is the only alternative to no solicitor at all, but it is a sad comment on our learned friends that it seems that, for some people, the only way to get hold of a lawyer is to hand him a pretty safe bet of a case and part with huge percentages of the proceeds for winning it.

* The Solicitor's Pro Bond Group may refer deserving cases to solicitors prepared to pursue them, for free. Use this service only for good not evil. 020 7929 5601.

If you are paying a solicitor, don't use them as a friend. Write down facts, names, addresses, and never chat on the phone. If they ask how you are, say 'Fine' even if you're dying; the meter's ticking and you may be charged for exchanging pleasantries. It's cheaper to fax your queries and write your own letters, based on their advice, always remembering to write 'Without Prejudice' at the top of any communication which could be used against you. Never putting anything on paper that you wouldn't wish to hear read out in front of your sainted grandmother is a very good tip in law and life.

Solicitors are supposed to give you written costs for each job, but they rarely do. If a solicitor overcharges, the following, kindly supplied by Vanessa Ward, may help:

> The agreement reached as to your agreed remuneration was not in writing pursuant to Section 57(3) of the Solicitors Act 1974 and therefore the agreement is not enforceable against me.

> I should like to draw your attention to Rule 15b(i) and (ii) of the Solicitors Practice Rules 1990 as revised in February 1991 by the Council of the Law Society (no. 13.08 of the Guide to the Professional Court of Solicitors, sixth edition, page 284). I did not receive from you either confirmation of my instructions in writing or a record of the agreed fee, as recommended. It is your duty to clarify any agreement as to the payment of your costs.

If still not happy, threaten to complain to the Office for the Supervision of Solicitors (01926 820082), who may look the bill over (called 'taxing') and make the solicitor cut it down. Solicitors hate this; it involves time and fuss, and they will probably make an offer to get you to go away.

From a friend comes the tip that if you are ever charged with a serious offence, don't just settle for the first barrister recommended. Go and watch a few in action first.

* **_The Legal Profession_, £55 as a book, £65 as a CD-rom, published by Chambers, 020 7606 1300, will help you choose by grouping solicitors and barristers by their specialisation, e.g. pensions, banking, personal injury. Order it from your lending library.**

MR THRIFTY RAISES FUNDS.

Turn your home into a film location

Not just for very grand houses; one lady makes a healthy sporadic income by renting her late husband's garage out, with all the tools just as he left it. Film and TV companies look for places close to their headquarters, so nobody has to stay in expensive hotels, and with lots of parking for their huge vans.

Production companies pay between £500 to £3000 a day to use your home, though it's harder work than it looks. One owner advises putting down duckboards over your lawn so that it is not ruined by people tramping all over it, and making a 'before' photo of the room in case anything is broken or missing later.

Not to be confused with letting a magazine photograph your lovely decor, for which there is no fee, nor with allowing a TV company to rampage around your home without first agreeing a fee, nor with letting *Hello!* magazine or similar photograph your celebrity wedding for megabucks.

* British Film Commission, 020 7460 5043. Lavish Locations, 020 8742 2992 Or try Strutt & Parker estate agents, 01635 521707.

The Historic Houses Association helps by selling a standard contract which you can personalise by adding requests like 'please wear gloves when moving furniture'. You can get this from Norman Hudson, High Wardington House, Upper Wardington, Banbury, Oxfordshire, OX17 1SP. 01295 750750. Norman will also personally handle contracts.

Market research

Market research companies pay around £25 to sit in a group in someone's home discussing the burning questions of the day, or what kind of cat food your pet prefers or whatever. Call market research companies in *Yellow Pages* and ask.

Be paid for shopping

Mystery Shoppers assess service standards in hotels and restaurants. You must have a phone, car and be prepared to work occasionally rather than regularly. NOP, 01865 260 300; Scher International, 125 High Holborn, London, WC1V 6QA.

Get a lodger

Under the Rent a Room scheme, if there is a
connecting door between your home and the
lodger's room, even if it is permanently locked,
you qualify as a landlady, male or female, and
you can take up to £4250 rent per year without
having to declare it or pay tax.

Pawning your valuables

We think of pawnbrokers, distinguished by the
three golden balls outside their shops, as quaint
remnants of cockney culture. But if you need
anything from £5 to £5000 fast, they are extremely
useful.

Pawning a valuable, like a watch or ring, involves
giving it in exchange for cash. You have to repay
the cash with interest within six months or the
pawnbroker keeps your gold. Or these days, it
can be anything: cars, paintings, antiques, TVs,
computers. It helps if you know how much you
want to borrow when you walk in. 'Can you lend
me £50 on this?' is the question to ask. The broker
asks for ID like a driving licence, decides that
you're not handing over stolen goods, then gives
you a contract to sign. Avoid brokers who charge
a setting-up fee.

It's safer than you think, as pawnbroking is
regulated by the Consumer Credit Act. It can
even be cheaper than a bank loan, if you need

short-term money, because there are no large setting-up fees, early payment penalties or long waits for a Yes or No. 'We're the last line of defence for many people,' one pointed out to me.

You pay interest each month, which is higher than credit cards charge, but they don't charge interest on the interest as credit cards do. If you haven't redeemed your 'pledge' by six months, you receive a warning letter that the goods will be sold. Once sold, the broker must write and tell you, sending the balance of the profit to you after deducting interest.

* Harvey and Thompson is a reputable national chain, 020 8692 0573. Make sure your pawnbroker is a member of the National Pawnbrokers Association, who will send you a list of members and sort out grievances. 1 Bell Yard, London, WC2A 2JP. 020 7242 1114.

Asking is free – charity grants

A friend was left penniless with two children, but educated both in top public schools with the aid of obscure charities. She adds that even Eton has subsidised places, but the poor but deserving don't think of applying. A shame; they want good brains. You can approach the school of your choice direct and ask.

If you hit hard times, it's comforting to know that there are funds to help. The *Charities Digest* makes fascinating reading, being the list of all British charities and what they do. The Koettgen Memorial Fund gives grants to British-born students to study commercial subjects. The Theatrical Ladies' Guild helps anyone who ever worked in the theatre, even selling programmes. Wireless to the Bedridden provides free radio and TV to the housebound or elderly. See what you can find that applies to you. Thousands of pounds in legacies are left that can't find any recipients.

* The *Charities Digest* costs £21.95, p+p free from Waterlow Professional Publishing, 6-14 Underwood Street, London N1 7JQ. 020 7490 0049. Or look it up in a reference library.

MR THRIFTY'S MONEY BOX

Taxing times

If you have trouble with tax collectors, ask for Customer Services at your Inland Revenue office. They may allow you extra time to pay if you have been a good payer in the past.

Not many people know that different tax inspectors will offer different deals. If you don't like the deal you're offered, politely say you'll consider it, then phone in again and ask to talk to someone else or a supervisor.

This also works with Sky TV, London Electricity and British Gas, all of whom initially insist that they have no way of reducing payments, letting you off charges etc. until you talk to someone who lets the cat out of the bag.

Free advice

TaxAid is a small charity offering free independent advice from specialists on tax and tax debt, to those who can't afford to pay for it.

Citizens Advice Bureaux don't have the specialists to answer complex tax queries; the Inland Revenue, by definition, isn't independent.

TaxAid advises on problems like tax demands, arrears, codes, self-employed accounts, appeals, refunds, investigations and Revenue errors and maladministration. In one case, a man who had been in hospital and couldn't do his administration found himself threatened with bankruptcy over an estimated £11,000 tax bill. TaxAid helped him to appeal, claim allowances and reduce the bill to £2000, paid by instalments.

* Linburn House, 342 Kilburn High Road, London NW6 2QJ. For a consultation, call 020 7624 3768 between 10 and 12am, Monday to Thursday.

Get an independent financial adviser

Such firms as Prudential, Barclays, Halifax, Legal & General, Abbey Life, Allied Dunbar and Pearl employ salespeople to sell only their plans. Talk to independent financial advisers, especially ones linked in networks, who use their buying power to get better deals, like DBS and Countrywide.

* Get the names of three local IFAs from IFAP Ltd, 17–19 Emery Road, Bristol, BS4 5PF. 0117 971 1177. www.ifap.org.uk/find.contact.htm; or try Investor Intelligence, 0500 10 10 14.

In my opinion you are best off talking to an independent financial adviser whom you pay by the hour. This is expensive, but a good way of getting the best advice, since you can never be sure that an independent adviser who is paid commission on what s/he sells is not swayed by less than ethical considerations about how much their commission might be.

A paid-upfront adviser then refunds you the commission paid by the investment company to whom you have given your money. This can be substantial, running into thousands. If you have bought a pension, the money must go back into the pension pot; it is illegal to pension-strip, as it's called. You can get the money back on other investments as a cheque, but you must pay tax on it.

The Institute of Financial Planning's members are all pay-as-you-go independent financial advisers. Ask for the Registry, or list.

* Whitefriars Centre, Lewins Mead, Bristol, BS1 2NT.
0117 930 4434.

www.moneyextra.com is an online service which makes independent comparisons of financial products for you.

DIY investment clubs

There are around three thousand seven hundred

investment clubs in Britain, of up to 20 members each. Members put in a monthly sum, perhaps £25, which is used to buy stocks and shares, with members controlling where cash is invested.

ProShare Investment Clubs is the non-profit-making national association of investment clubs and produces a manual on setting up your club, at £28. New clubs get the first year's membership of the club free, a magazine and access to a query hotline. Companies like Barclays Stockbrokers, Charles Schwab and YorkSHARE (the Yorkshire Building Society) run special services for investment clubs.

* ProShare, 020 7394 5200.

Considerable discounts to shareholders

Shareholders have only one certainty: that you will be invited to shareholders' meetings at which there is a good buffet and free drinks, to put you in a good mood.

However badly your shares perform, if you put cash into companies, you get wonderful extra perks, more valuable than your shares in some cases. For instance, at the time of writing, 500 ordinary shares in First Choice Holidays brings you 10 per cent off your First Choice or Sovereign holiday from the special Shareholders' Helpline. Five hundred shares in Next brings 25 per cent off all purchases. Some perks have time limits, and the cost of buying and selling shares adds to the price of your perk.

* These and huge numbers more are listed in *The Shareholders' Perks Guide*, free from Hargreaves Lansdown, 0117 988 9880.

To check a company's standing before investing, ask the Financial Services Authority. It also has an information officer to answer specific queries at 0800 606 1234.

* 25 North Colonnade, Canary Wharf, London E14 5HS.

MR THRIFTY TAKES A FINAL BOW

The cost of funerals makes you weep. Your family may need that money to live on. You can save money if you plan ahead. Specify your desires; your family won't feel strong enough to shop around or be creative after you die.

Rather than paying into a funeral plan, it may be cheaper to put aside a sum in an Egg or building society account in the name of the funeral organiser, otherwise the money will be frozen on your death.

Some local councils (like Wigan) have negotiated cut-price funerals for residents. Call your local cemetery (listed in the phone book under the council) and ask.

Woodland burial grounds

Cremation is cheaper than a grave. You can be buried in your back garden, but it will reduce the property value. Get advice from the Environment Agency 0845 933 3111. Better still are the new Woodland Burial Grounds, over a hundred in

Britain. Each offers you the chance to return your body to Nature in beautiful surroundings, at a moderate cost. Greenhaven, near Rugby, for instance, charges £490 to collect a body from London, take it to the ground, dig the grave, bury you in an eco-coffin provided, and plant a tree over the grave which is tended. More details of this and all other aspects of death are in the *New Natural Death Handbook*, £11.65 including p&p from the Natural Death Centre, 20 Heber Road, London, NW2 6AA. 020 8208 2853.

Cheapest Coffins

The cheapest cardboard coffin costs £20 plus £12 overnight delivery, from Celtic Caskets, 01283 521104. The same company runs a funeral service, Green Undertakings (UK) in Burton-on-Trent, which I must stress is not associated with a Watchet-based namelike. The UK company offers free advice, lots of DIY coffin accessories including a kit to paint at £75 p&p free, and all or parts of funerals (like dealing with the body) throughout Britain, including horse-drawn carriages at £500.

People think they can save all these costs by donating their bodies for medical research. Only a few bodies are accepted. You must be whole, non-cancerous and within easy reach of a medical school. HM Inspector of Anatomy, 133–155 Waterloo Road, London, SE1 8UG (020

7972 4342) or your local medical school will give details.

If you are not religious, the British Humanist Association will send a trained representative to act as master or mistress of ceremonies at level-pegging prices to a churchman. If a relative wants to conduct a service, they have a helpful booklet called *Funerals without God* by Jane Wynne Wilson with sample texts and poetry.

* 47 Theobalds Road, London, WC1X 8SP. 020 7430 0908.

Making a will

Keep banks, building societies and lawyers away from this unless you have complications like a farm changing hands. They will charge whacking great fees and take too long.

I am not over-impressed by willmaking services. Many aim to make money long-term by charging you for storage; they can get quite unpleasant if you resist and say, 'I'm putting my will in a fireproof box at home instead,' which is your cheaper option.

You can make your own will by filling in a Willmaker kit available from stationers at under £10. Most charities offer free advice and guides, not to mention Legacy Officers to help you (that's with big charities like Oxfam).

If you suspect someone is likely to challenge your will after your death, it is a good idea to leave a charity some money, professional willmaker Stewart Smith points out. Then, if your will is questioned, the charity will employ professionals to fight for itself, and incidentally your other legatees.

Appoint two younger friends as executors. It will enable them to fill in the probate application, which they need to release your assets to your heirs, if you keep your affairs in apple-pie order, with a master list of what you own or owe to hand.

For further Thrifty tips:
www.mrthrifty.co.uk